PSYCHOPATHY:

Theory and Research

APPROACHES TO
BEHAVIOR PATHOLOGY SERIES
Brendan Maher — Series Editor

PSYCHOPATHY:

Theory and Research

ROBERT D. HARE

University of British Columbia

John Wiley & Sons, Inc.

New York · London · Sydney · Toronto

Library of Congress Catalogue Card Number: 79-120704

ISBN 0-471-35146-6 Cloth
ISBN 0-471-35147-4 Paper

Printed in the United States of America

10 9 8 7 6 5 4 3

SERIES PREFACE

Abnormal psychology may be studied in many different ways. One traditional method of approach emphasizes the description of clinical syndromes with an extensive use of case histories to illustrate the central phenomena and the psychological processes believed to underlie them. Another common position is found in the adoption of a systematic theory (such as psychodynamic or behavioral) as a framework within which important problems of abnormal psychology may be delineated and interpreted.

Whether systematic or eclectic, descriptive or interpretive, the teaching of a course in abnormal psychology faces certain difficult problems. Similar to other areas of science, abnormal psychology has exhibited a rapid increase in knowledge and in the rate at which new knowledge is being acquired. It is becoming more and more difficult for the college teacher to keep abreast of contemporary developments over as wide a range of subjects as abnormal psychology encompasses. Even in the areas of his personal interest and special competence the instructor may be hard pressed to cover significant concepts and findings with real comprehensiveness.

Adding to this spate of new knowledge is the fact that, in the field of abnormal psychology, we are witnessing a resurgence of enthusiasm for empirical research of an experimental kind together with a growth of interest in deviant behavior on the part of other scientists, notably the geneticists, neurobiologists, biochemists on the one hand and epidemiologists, anthropologists and social scientists on the other. It is less and less possible to claim mastery of a topic area in abnormal psychology when approaching it purely from the standpoint of a single psychological theory. An adequate understanding of any central topic now depends on familiarity with literature coming from many quarters of the scientific community.

Knowledge multiplies but time does not. Working within the limits of forty to fifty lecture hours available for the usual course in general abnormal psychology, it has become necessary for the student to turn more and more often to specialized outside reading to acquire the depth that cannot be given by any one textbook or by any one instructor. Although much can be gained by reading a range of selected reprints, these are often written originally for audiences other than the undergraduates and for purposes too narrowly technical to be entirely suited to instruction.

The present volume is one of a series developed to meet the need for depth of coverage in the central topic areas of abnormal psychology. The series is prepared with certain criteria in mind. Each volume has been planned to be scientifically authoritative, to be written with the clarity and directness necessary for the introductory student, but with a sophistication and timeliness of treatment that should render it of value to the advanced student and the fellow-specialist. Selection of the topics to be included in the series has been guided by a decision to concentrate on problem areas that are systematically and empirically important: in each case there are significant theoretical problems to be examined and a body of research literature to cast light on the several solutions that are adduced. Although it is anticipated that the student may read one or more of these volumes in addition to a standard text, the total series will cover the major part of a typical course in abnormal psychology and could well be used in place of a single text.

We are in a period of exciting growth and change in abnormal psychology. Concepts and hypotheses that have dominated the field for over half a century are giving place to new and provocative viewpoints. Much of this has been accomplished in one short decade: it is clear that the character of the field will be changed even more radically in the decades to come. It is the hope of the editor and the contributors to this series that they will play a useful part in preparing the coming generation of psychopathologists for the challenge of the years that lie ahead.

Brendan Maher

PREFACE

This book represents an experimental psychologist's approach to the study of psychopathy, a behavioral disorder and social problem just beginning to receive the attention it deserves from scientifically oriented investigators. After discussing the concept of psychopathy, I have surveyed and integrated the relevant theory and research findings and have attempted to develop new hypotheses and to offer some suggestions for future research. Although representative coverage is given to the literature from various fields and disciplines, my own interests and attitudes toward research in abnormal behavior are evident. As a result, I have emphasized on theory and research having to do with the psychophysiological, learning, and socialization processes thought to be associated with the disorder. I recognize, of course, that other approaches are possible and desirable.

The book is intended for graduate and undergraduate students in abnormal psychology, personality, and clinical psychology, and for investigators in the field of abnormal behavior. It should also be of interest to students taking courses in criminology, social work, mental health, and the sociology of deviance, as well as to those who must deal with psychopaths in the course of their work. Included in this latter category are clinical psychologists, psychiatrists, counselors, social workers, probation officers, and correctional personnel.

The preparation of this book, as well as some of the research reported herein, was facilitated by Public Health Research Grant 609-7-163 from the Canadian National Health Grants Program, by a Leave Fellowship (1969–1970) from the Canada Council, and by a research award from the Canadian Mental Health Association.

I thank those who helped in the preparation of the manuscript: particularly my wife, Averil, who did most of the library research, provided encouragement, and, along with Mrs. Marie Donald, did the typing; Mrs. Arlen Sue Fox of Wiley, whose efforts were extensive and helpful; and Dr. Daisy Schalling of the Karolinska Institute, Stockholm, who read and commented on the manuscript in its final stages.

Robert D. Hare

CONTENTS

PSYCHOPATHY:

Theory and Research

CHAPTER ONE

THE CONCEPT OF PSYCHOPATHY

It seems appropriate to begin a book on psychopathy with a case history illustrating some of the characteristics generally associated with the disorder, and to mention some of the definitions currently in use. Of necessity, the account to be given is brief and incomplete, and represents the pattern of behavior exhibited by only one individual. For detailed clinical accounts of psychopathy and its various manifestations, the reader is referred to Cleckley's excellent book *The Mask of Sanity* (1964). Information on the historical development of the concept of psychopathy can be found in Craft (1965), Maughs (1941), and McCord and McCord (1964).

CASE HISTORY OF A PSYCHOPATH

Donald S., 30 years old, has just completed a three-year prison term for fraud, bigamy, false pretenses, and escaping lawful custody. The circumstances leading up to these offenses are interesting and consistent with his past behavior. With less than a month left to serve on an earlier 18-month term for fraud, he faked illness and escaped from the prison hospital. During the ten months of freedom that followed he engaged in a variety of illegal enterprises; the activity that resulted in his recapture was typical of his method of operation. By passing himself off as the "field executive" of an international philanthropic foundation, he was able to enlist the aid of several religious organizations in a fund-raising campaign. The campaign moved slowly at first, and in an attempt to speed things up, he arranged an interview with the local TV station. His performance during the interview was so impressive that funds started to pour in. However, unfortunately for Donald, the interview was also carried on a national news network. He was recognized and quickly arrested. During the ensuing trial it became evident that he experienced no sense of wrongdoing for his activities. He maintained, for example, that his passionate plea for funds "primed the pump"—that is, induced people to give to other charities as well as to the one he professed to represent. At the same time, he stated that most donations to charity are made by those who feel guilty about something and who therefore deserve to be bilked. This ability to rationalize his behavior and his lack of self-criticism were also evident in his attempts to solicit aid from the very people he had misled. Perhaps it is a tribute to his persuasiveness that a number of individuals actually did come to his support. During his three-year prison term, Donald spent much time searching for legal loopholes and writing to outside authorities, including local lawyers, the Prime Minister of Canada, and a Canadian representative to the United Nations. In each case he verbally attacked them for representing the authority and injustice responsible for his predicament. At the same time he requested them to intercede on his behalf and in the name of the justice they professed to represent.

While in prison he was used as a subject in some of the author's research. On his release he applied for admission to a university and, by way of reference, told the registrar that he had been one of the author's research colleagues! Several months later the author received a letter from him requesting a letter of recommendation on behalf of Donald's application for a job.

Donald was the youngest of three boys born to middle-class parents. Both of his brothers led normal, productive lives. His father spent a great deal of time with his business; when he was home he tended to be moody and to drink heavily when things were not going right. Donald's mother was a gentle, timid woman who tried to please her husband and to maintain a semblance of family harmony. When she discovered her children engaged in some mischief, she would threaten to tell their father. However, she seldom carried out these threats because she did not want to disturb her husband and because his reactions were likely to be dependent on his mood at the time; on some occasions he would fly into a rage and beat the children and on others he would administer a verbal reprimand, sometimes mild and sometimes severe.

By all accounts Donald was considered a willful and difficult child.

When his desire for candy or toys was frustrated he would begin with a show of affection, and if this failed he would throw a temper tantrum; the latter was seldom necessary because his angelic appearance and artful ways usually got him what he wanted. Similar tactics were used to avoid punishment for his numerous misdeeds. At first he would attempt to cover up with an elaborate facade of lies, often shifting the blame to his brothers. If this did not work, he would give a convincing display of remorse and contrition. When punishment was unavoidable he would become sullenly defiant, regarding it as an unjustifiable tax on his pleasures.

Although he was obviously very intelligent, his school years were academically undistinguished. He was restless, easily bored, and frequently truant. His behavior in the presence of the teacher or some other authority was usually quite good, but when he was on his own he generally got himself or others into trouble. Although he was often suspected of being the culprit, he was adept at talking his way out of difficulty.

Donald's misbehavior as a child took many forms including lying, cheating, petty theft, and the bullying of smaller children. As he grew older he became more and more interested in sex, gambling, and alcohol. When he was 14 he made crude sexual advances toward a younger girl, and when she threatened to tell her parents he locked her in a shed. It was about 16 hours before she was found. Donald at first denied knowledge of the incident, later stating that she had seduced him and that the door must have locked itself. He expressed no concern for the anguish experienced by the girl and her parents, nor did he give any indication that he felt morally culpable for what he had done. His parents were able to prevent charges being brought against him. Nevertheless, incidents of this sort were becoming more frequent and, in an attempt to prevent further embarrassment to the family, he was sent away to a private boarding school. His academic work there was of uneven quality, being dependent on his momentary interests. Nevertheless, he did well at individual competitive sports and public debating. He was a source of excitement for many of the other boys, and was able to think up interesting and unusual things to do. Rules and regulations were considered a meaningless hindrance to his self-expression, but he violated them so skillfully that it was often difficult to prove that he had actually done so. The teachers described him as an "operator" whose behavior was determined entirely by the possibility of attaining what he wanted—in most cases something that was concrete, immediate, and personally relevant.

When he was 17, Donald left the boarding school, forged his father's name to a large check, and spent about a year traveling around the world. He apparently lived well, using a combination of charm, physical attractiveness, and false pretenses to finance his way. During subsequent years he held a succession of jobs, never staying at any one for more than a few months. Throughout this period he was charged with a variety of crimes, including theft, drunkenness in a public place, assault, and many traffic violations. In most cases he was either fined or given a light sentence.

His sexual experiences were frequent, casual, and callous. When he was 22 he married a 41-year-old woman whom he had met in a bar. Several other marriages followed, all bigamous. In each case the pattern was the same: he would marry someone on impulse, let her support him for several months, and then leave. One marriage was particularly interesting. After being charged with fraud Donald was sent to a psychiatric institution for a period of observation. While there he came to the attention of a female member of the professional staff. His charm, physical attractiveness, and convincing promises to reform led her to intervene on his behalf. He was given a suspended sentence and they were married a week later. At first things went reasonably well, but when she refused to pay some of his gambling debts he forged her name to a check and left. He was soon caught and given an 18-month prison term. As mentioned earlier, he escaped with less than a month left to serve.

It is interesting to note that Donald sees nothing particularly wrong with his behavior, nor does he express remorse or guilt for using others and causing them grief. Although his behavior is self-defeating in the long run, he considers it to be practical and possessed of good sense. Periodic punishments do nothing to decrease his egotism and confidence in his own abilities, nor do they offset the often considerable short-term gains of which he is capable. However, these short-term gains are invariably obtained at the expense of someone else. In this respect his behavior is entirely egocentric, and his needs are satisfied without any concern for the feelings and welfare of others.

DESCRIPTIONS OF THE PSYCHOPATH

The current American Psychiatric Association term for the individual described in the case history is *sociopathic personality disturbance, antisocial reaction,* defined by the Diagnostic and Statistical Manual of Mental Disorders (1952) as follows:

> This term refers to chronically antisocial individuals who are always in trouble, profiting neither from experience nor punishment, and maintaining no real loyalties to any person, group or code. They are frequently callous and hedonistic, showing marked emotional immaturity, with lack of responsibility, lack of judgment, and an ability to rationalize their behavior so that it appears warranted, reasonable, and justified (p. 38).

The term is cumbersome to use and in practice is sometimes replaced by *sociopath* or *sociopathic personality*. However, the older and more familiar term *psychopath* still retains its popularity, and is generally used to refer to the diagnostic category just described.

The Group for the Advancement of Psychiatry has proposed that the term *tension-discharge disorder, impulse-ridden personality* be used in place of psychopathy or sociopathy when dealing with children, since the latter terms imply a personality pattern that is too fixed to apply to most children. The impulse-ridden personality is described as follows:

> These children show shallow relationships with adults or other children, having very low frustration tolerance. They exhibit great difficulty in control of their impulses, both aggressive and sexual, which are discharged immediately and impulsively, without delay or inhibition, and often with little regard for the consequences. Little anxiety, internalized conflict, or guilt is experienced by most of these children, as the conflict remains largely external, between society and their impulses. . . . The basic defect in impulse controls appears to be reinforced by a deficit in conscience or superego formation, with failure to develop the capacity for tension-storage and for the postponement of gratifications. . . . Although their judgment and time concepts are poor, they usually have adequate intelligence and their reality testing in certain areas is quite effective (Group for the Advancement of Psychiatry, 1966).

Cleckley (1964) has provided the most detailed clinical accounts of psychopathy and its many manifestations. On the basis of his extensive experience, he outlined what he considered to be the main features of the disorder: superficial charm and good intelligence; absence of delusions and other signs of irrational thinking; absence of "nervousness" or neurotic manifestations; unreliability; untruthfulness and insincerity; lack of remorse or shame; antisocial behavior without apparent compunction; poor judgment and failure to learn from experience; pathologic egocentricity and incapacity for love; general poverty in major affective reactions; specific loss of insight; unresponsiveness in general interpersonal relations; fantastic and uninviting behavior with drink and sometimes without; suicide threats rarely carried out; sex life impersonal, trivial, and poorly integrated; failure to follow any life plan. The first three characteristics are positive in nature and serve to emphasize the fact that the psychopath's behavior is not simply the manifestation of disturbed mental functioning. According to Cleckley, the psychopath lacks the ability to experience the emotional components of personal and interpersonal behavior—he mimics the human personality but is unable to really *feel*. Thus, although his verbalizations (for example, "I'm sorry I got you in trouble") appear normal, they are devoid of emotional meaning, a disorder that Cleckley has termed *semantic dementia*. As Johns and Quay (1962) so aptly stated it, the psychopath knows the words but not the music, with the result that he is unable to show empathy or genuine concern for others. He manipulates and uses others to satisfy his own demands; yet, through a glib sophistication and superficial sincerity, he is often able to convince those he has used and harmed of his innocence or his intentions to change.

Karpman (1961) described the psychopath as a callous, emotionally immature, two-dimensional person without any real depth. His emotional reactions are simple and animal-like, occurring only with immediate frustrations and discomfort. However, he is able to *simulate* emotional reactions and affectional attachments when it will help him to obtain what he wants from others. He experiences neither the psychological nor the physiological aspects of anxiety or fear, although he may react with something resembling fear when his immediate comfort is threatened. His social and sexual relations with others are superficial but demanding and manipulative. Future rewards and punishments do not exist, except in an abstract manner, with the result that they have no effect on his immediate behavior. His judgment is poor and his behavior is often guided by impulse and current needs; he is therefore constantly in trouble. His attempts to extricate himself often produce an intricate and contradictory web of blatant lies, coupled with theatrical and often convincing explanations and promises.

Karpman considered psychopaths to be of either the *aggressive-predatory* or the *passive-parasitic type*. The former refers to the psychopathic individual who satisfies his needs by extremely aggressive and callous predatoriness, actively taking what he wants. The second type refers to the psychopath who gets what he wants by the parasitic "bleeding" of others, often by appearing as a helpless individual in need of infinite amounts of help and sympathy.

Arieti (1967) also described several types of psychopathy, including the *simple* and the *complex*. The simple psychopath's main characteristic is an inability to delay the gratification of psychological and biological needs, no matter what the future consequences to himself or to others. On an intellectual level, he knows that he could satisfy his needs by using the long-term processes normally necessary for the mature and socially acceptable attainment of goals. However, the future exists in only a vague, faint way and it has no immediate emotional significance for him. As a result, he is unwilling to delay gratification of his needs. Moreover, the possibility of future punishment for his actions fails to have any effect on his immediate behavior since he is unable to experience what Arieti terms "long-circuited anxiety," a vague expectation of some possible danger or discomfort. In other words, the immediate emotional consequences of anticipated punishment are not sufficient to make the psychopath inhibit his present behavior. Whatever anxiety he experiences is of a "short-circuited" nature —a reaction to immediate tension or discomfort—a point made in a slightly different way by Cleckley and Karpman.

The complex psychopath, according to Arieti, is similar to the simple psychopath, but his behavior is guided not only by need gratification but also by how to do what he wants and get away with it. Such psychopaths are usually very intelligent and able to plan methods of getting what they want without any regard for social morality. Professional bank robbers and some unscrupulous politicians and businessmen could be included within this category, along with some of the psychopaths described by Cleckley.

Most clinical descriptions of the psychopath make some sort of reference to his egocentricity, lack of empathy, and inability to form warm, emotional relationships with others—characteristics that lead him to treat others as objects instead of as persons and prevent him from experiencing guilt and remorse for having done so. After an extensive review of the literature, McCord and McCord (1964) concluded that the two essential features of psychopathy are *lovelessness* and *guiltlessness*. Similarly, Craft (1965) considered the two primary features of psychopathy to be a lack of feeling, affection, or love for others and a tendency to act on impulse and without forethought. Secondary features, stemming from these two, are aggressiveness, lack of shame or guilt, inability to profit from experience, and a lack of appropriate motivation.

Both Foulds (1965) and Buss (1966) considered egocentricity and lack of empathy to be largely responsible for the psychopath's disturbed interpersonal relations. Being unable to place himself in another person's position, the psychopath is able to manipulate others as he would any other object. He can therefore achieve satisfaction of his own needs without concern for the effects that his actions will have. And, lacking the ability to take the role of other persons, the psychopath is unable to anticipate what their reactions to his unusual behavior will be.

Neurotic "Psychopathy"

Psychopaths are obviously not the only ones who engage in antisocial behavior. Many antisocial and aggressive acts, for example, are committed by individuals who are suffering from severe emotional disturbances or who are experiencing unbearable frustrations and inner conflicts. Since their antisocial behavior is symptomatic of a more basic emotional problem, these individuals are sometimes referred to as *symptomatic, secondary,* or *neurotic* psychopaths (see Karpman, 1961).[1] Other terms that have been used include *acting-out neurotic, neurotic delinquent,* and *neurotic*

[1] Correspondingly, the "true" psychopath, that is, the individual discussed in this book, is sometimes referred to as the *primary, idiopathic,* or *classical psychopath.*

character. The Group for the Advancement of Psychiatry has suggested that the term *neurotic personality disorder* be used when dealing with children.

One of the difficulties with terms such as secondary and neurotic "psychopathy" is that they imply that individuals so labeled are basically psychopaths. However, this is likely to be misleading because the motivations behind their behavior, as well as their personality structure, life history, response to treatment, and prognosis, are very different from those of the psychopath. Moreover, unlike psychopaths, these individuals experience guilt and remorse for their behavior, and are able to form meaningful, affectional relationships with others. Since the antisocial actions of these individuals are motivated by neurotic conflicts and tensions, it may be more appropriate to use terms that emphasize the neurotic element in their behavior, for example, acting-out neurotic, neurotic delinquent.

Many individuals exhibit aggressive, antisocial behavior, not because they are psychopathic or emotionally disturbed, but because they have grown up in a delinquent subculture or in an environment that fosters and rewards such behavior. Their behavior, although considered deviant by society's standards, is nevertheless consonant with that of their own group, gang, or family. The terms used for these individuals include *dyssocial "psychopath," subcultural delinquent,* and, when children are involved, *sociosyntonic personality disorder* (Group for the Advancement of Psychiatry). Unlike the "true" psychopath, these individuals are capable of strong loyalties and warm relationships with members of their own group (for instance, criminal organizations, delinquent gangs).

Statistical Studies

It is of considerable interest that the clinical subdivision of antisocial behavior into psychopathic, neurotic, and subcultural components is supported by several statistical studies of case-history data, behavior ratings, and questionnaire responses. Using case-history data, Jenkins and his associates (1964, 1966) have repeatedly isolated several clusters of personality traits (or syndromes) occurring in delinquent children and in guidance clinic referrals. The three most common clusters have been labeled the *unsocialized-aggressive syndrome* (psychopathic: assaultive tendencies, starting fights, cruelty, defiance of authority, malicious mischief, inadequate guilt feelings), the *overanxious syndrome* (neurotic: seclusiveness, shyness, apathy, worrying, sensitiveness, submissiveness), and the *socialized delinquency syndrome* (subcultural: bad companions, gang activities, cooperative stealing, habitual truancy from school and home, out late at night).

Other studies have produced results very similar to those obtained by Jenkins. Thus a series of studies using behavior ratings (Quay, 1964b), case-history data (Quay, 1964a), and responses to questionnaires (Peterson, Quay, & Tiffany, 1961), has consistently yielded at least two main factors (groups of related characteristics) related to delinquency. The first factor, labeled *psychopathic delinquency,* reflects tough, amoral, and rebellious qualities coupled with impulsivity, distrust of authority, and freedom from family ties. The second factor, labeled *neurotic delinquency,* also reflects impulsive and aggressive tendencies; however, in this case they are associated with tension, guilt, remorse, depression, and discouragement. A third factor has been identified in studies of personality questionnaires (Peterson, Quay, & Tiffany, 1961). Labeled *subcultural delinquency,* the factor reflects the attitudes and values commonly believed to occur in delinquent groups; it is similar to Jenkins's socialized delinquency syndrome and the dyssocial "psychopath" described above.

The results of several studies by Finney (see, for example, 1966) provide further support for the distinction between psychopathic and neurotic forms of antisocial behavior. Using responses to a personality inventory, the MMPI (see p. 15), Finney isolated several factors, including one related to antisocial behavior and another related to anxiety, distress, and guilt. On the basis of his findings, Finney was able to distinguish between psychopathy (high in antisocial behavior, low in guilt), acting-out neurosis (high in antisocial behavior, high in guilt), neurotic inhibition (low in antisocial behavior, high in guilt), and normalcy (low in antisocial behavior, low in guilt).

THE DIAGNOSIS OF PSYCHOPATHY

Psychiatrists who have worked extensively with psychopaths are in basic agreement concerning at least the main descriptive features of this group. In order to assess the degree of agreement among psychiatrists in general, Gray and Hutchison (1964) mailed a questionnaire to 937 Canadian psychiatrists. The main portion of the questionnaire was a 29-item list of traits and features generally used to describe psychopaths. The psychiatrists were asked to rank in order the ten items they felt were most important in the diagnosis of the psychopathic personality. Of the 677 who responded, 89.3 percent felt that the concept of psychopathic personality was a meaningful one. They considered the following features to be most significant in the diagnosis of psychopathy: (1) does not profit from experience; (2) lacks a sense of responsibility; (3) unable to form meaningful relationships; (4) lacks control over impulses; (5) lacks moral sense; (6) chronically or recurrently antisocial; (7) punishment does not alter behavior; (8) emotionally immature; (9) unable to experience guilt; and (10) self-centered. Some other responses were of interest. For example, 14.4 percent of the respondents thought that psychopathy was primarily genetic in nature, 38.2 percent thought that it was primarily environmental, and 43.9 percent considered both genetic and environmental factors important. Although only 12.7 percent thought that the disorder could be diagnosed before the age of eight, 78.5 percent stated that a diagnosis could be made by the age of 18.

These findings are of interest because they represent the views of a large segment of the psychiatric profession (at least in Canada). Also of interest is the way in which the concept of psychopathy is actually used by psychiatrists and psychologists engaged in research on the topic. Albert, Brigante, and Chase (1959) subjected 70 articles on psychopathy to an intensive content analysis. They began with 75 descriptive statements of the psychopathic personality and scored each article on the basis of whether it mentioned a given characteristic as being present in psychopaths (1) to a greater degree, (2) to a lesser degree, or (3) to the same degree as in the general population. The results for those studies dealing with adults are shown in Table 1. They indicate that there is a considerable degree of agreement among researchers concerning the main characteristics of psychopaths. A similar degree of agreement was found in those studies dealing with psychopathic children (less than 16 years). In this case, the most consistent features were antisocial aggression; inadequate superego; inability to identify with others; low ego strength; narcissism; absence of conflict, anxiety, and guilt; temper tantrums; motor hyperactivity; and absence of goal-directed behavior.

Although there is reasonable agreement on what the term psychopathy means, it is not always easy to identify those individuals who warrant the label "psychopathic." In this respect, the concept shares a problem that is common to all psychiatric categories, namely, the problem of diagnostic reliability.

The reliability of psychiatric diagnosis is generally not very impressive (see Buss, 1966; Phillips, 1968; Zubin, 1967). Nevertheless, there are indications that it can be considerably increased when (1) the criteria for assignment of patients to the various categories are made as clear and explicit as possible; (2) biographical and psychometric data are available to supplement clinical interviews; and (3) allowances are made for the degree of disagreement involved. When these requirements are satisfied, the diagnostic reliability of some categories, most notably the brain syndromes and psychopathy, can be appreciable (Spitzer, Cohen, Fleiss, and Endicott, 1967). Hopefully, the type of research discussed in the present volume will help make the concept of psychopathy more precise and objective than it is at the present time.

TABLE 1: Mention of Some Characteristics as Present in Psychopaths to a Greater Degree, a Lesser Degree, or the Same Degree as in the General Population (After Albert et al., 1959.)

Characteristic	Greater Degree	Same Degree	Lesser Degree
Antisocial aggression	35		3
Recidivism and lawbreaking	29	1	
Conflict, anxiety	12	1	15
Inability to delay satisfaction	26		1
Inability to plan or use past experience	24	1	
Lack of insight	20	2	1
Narcissism	22		
Psychoticism	6		14
Neuroticism	5		15
Irresponsibility	19		
Goal-directed behavior			17
Emotional instability	16		1
Irresponsible sexual behavior	16		1
Intelligence	7	9	
Interpersonal sincerity			14
Emotional depth			13
Emotional maturity			13
Inadequate superego	13		
Morality			13
Lack of personality integration	12		
Hyperactive	10		1
Mood lability	11		
Alcoholism	9	1	
Ambition	1		9
Breadth of social contacts	3		6
Callousness	9		
Ego strength			9
Pathological lying	9		
Abnormal EEG	7		1

Typology Versus Dimension

There is some disagreement among clinicians and investigators about the most appropriate way of conceptualizing psychopathy. One viewpoint, implicit in the use of diagnostic categories or typologies, is that psychopathy is a relatively distinct clinical and behavioral entity—a specific combination or clustering of characteristics that, individually and in other combinations, may be found in other disorders and in normal persons.

However, many investigators find it more appealing to conceptualize behavior, normal and abnormal, in dimensional terms. According to this view, psychopaths as such do not exist, although some individuals may be considered more psychopathic than others if they occupy a more extreme position on some dimension that we choose to label "psychopathy." The difficulty here is that before we can really say that one person is more or less psychopathic than another, we need to know more about the makeup of the dimension. Assume, for example, that Person A exhibits all of the characteristics that we feel are relevant to the dimension of psychopathy, and that Person B exhibits only two-thirds of these characteristics. Who is the more psychopathic? If the dimension consists of the *number* of relevant characteristics, then Person A would be considered more psychopathic than B. However, suppose that the characteristics exhibited by B, though fewer in number, are more severe than those shown by A. Who is the more psychopathic now? The problem becomes even more complicated if we assume that the defining features of psychopathy, or for that matter any other complex dimension of behavior, are not equally weighted—that is, that some are more important than others. Under these conditions, an individual's position on the dimension can only be established when we know the number and severity of relevant characteristics exhibited, and the weights assigned them. In principle, it would be possible to use modern statistical techniques to obtain information of this sort, and to use it to yield a single score indicative of a given individual's degree of psychopathy.

Perhaps it is so difficult to decide whether psychopathy is best viewed as a typology or as a dimensional concept because both views are appropriate, representing, as it were, different sides of the same coin. Similarly, it is possible that "the conflict between typology and dimensionality is a pseudoconflict dependent upon the state of knowledge of the field," (Zubin, 1967, p. 398), and that research on psychopathy and other disorders of behavior can be fruitfully carried out without a formal commitment to a particular view.

CHAPTER TWO

PSYCHOMETRIC STUDIES
OF PSYCHOPATHY

The extensive clinical descriptions of the psychopath discussed in Chapter 1 have been supplemented and to a certain extent empirically tested by studies using a variety of psychometric devices. In this chapter we consider briefly a selection of these studies, particularly those that are concerned with the psychopath's personality and his intellectual processes.

INTELLIGENCE SCALES

A large number of studies with various forms of the *Wechsler-Bellevue Intelligence Scale* (see the recent bibliography by Hare and Hare, 1968, for a detailed list) strongly supports the clinical impression that psychopaths as a group have at least average global intelligence. Beyond this, many investigators have been concerned with Wechsler's (1958) contention that psychopaths generally obtain higher IQ scores on the performance portion of this test (for example, Block Design, Object Assembly, Picture Completion) than on the verbal portion (for instance, Vocabulary, Similarities, Comprehension). The results of these studies have been inconsistent, some supporting Wechsler's hypothesis (see, for example, Fisher, 1961; Manne, Kandel, and Rosenthal, 1962) and others failing to do so (see, for example, Craddick, 1961; Gurvitz, 1950).

Although the attempts to show that psychopaths and normal individuals differ intellectually have not been too successful, it is still possible that important differences will emerge with the use of tests specifically designed to measure the multitudinous dimensions of intelligence (Guilford, 1966). We may find, for instance, that the psychopath's tendency to disregard the commonly accepted rules and regulations is reflected in a capacity for *divergent thinking*—that is, for seeing things in novel and unusual ways, unhampered by the ordinary constraints.

Before concluding this section, we should consider the possibility that most estimates of the global intelligence of psychopaths have been conservative. Investigators have generally used subjects whose antisocial behavior was so persistent and/or poorly planned that they were sent either to a psychiatric institution for observation or to prison. Whether these psychopaths are less intelligent than those who manage to avoid being caught or convicted is not known, although we might suspect that this is indeed the case. If so it would probably mean that the *total* population of psychopaths is, on the average, more intelligent than the general population, at least as reflected in the standard tests of intelligence.

It is no doubt true that even those psychopaths who sometimes get caught are frequently successful at their antisocial enterprises. This periodic reinforcement could be partially responsible for the great persistence of their antisocial activities. We might expect that the really intelligent psychopaths, particularly those who are also charming and persuasive, would be even more successful at deviant activities. In many cases these individuals may even be a source of admiration and envy, since they frequently engage in enterprises that, although unethical and callous, are nevertheless legal (or quasi-legal) and very lucrative. And even if they are caught in some illegal act (such as fraud, embezzlement, swindling, or stock manipulation), the rewards may greatly outweigh the often meager punishments administered by society.

SELF-REPORT INVENTORIES

Most personality studies of psychopathy have used some form of self-report inventory. Unfortunately, their interpretation is made difficult by the possible presence of a number of factors other than test content. These *response-bias factors* include a tendency to endorse items that are considered "good" or desirable by society (*social desirability*) and a tendency to endorse items regardless of their content (*acquiescence*). A review of these and other response-bias factors can be found in Klein, Barr, and Wolitsky (1967).

It is very likely that studies involving criminal populations are considerably influenced by social desirability. In addition, it is quite possible that the psychopath's responses to the items on a personality test are influenced by his assessment of the testing situation and by his estimate of which responses are likely to do the most for him. Although there is as yet no empirical support for this suggestion, it is worth keeping in mind as we briefly review a sampling of personality studies.

Minnesota Multiphasic Personality Inventory

A number of studies of psychopathy have used the *Minnesota Multiphasic Personality Inventory* (*MMPI*), a widely used self-report inventory designed to differentiate among various psychiatric conditions (see Dahlstrom and Welsh, 1960). Strictly speaking, the studies that have used the MMPI really tell us very little about the personality structure of psychopaths. Instead, they tend more to test the ability of the MMPI to differentiate between various clinical groups. Viewed in this way, the results have been fairly consistent, with psychopaths generally obtaining MMPI profiles that are somewhat different from those obtained by normal subjects and other psychiatric groups (Dahlstrom and Welsh, 1960). There is also some evidence that the MMPI is able to differentiate (in a gross way) between psychopathic and nonpsychopathic criminals (Craddick, 1962; Hare, 1969; Silver, 1963). Figure 1, for example, illustrates the sort of MMPI profile obtained by penitentiary inmates involved in the present author's research. It is apparent that the two scales that differentiate best between psychopathic and nonpsychopathic criminals are the Psychopathic Deviate (*Pd*)

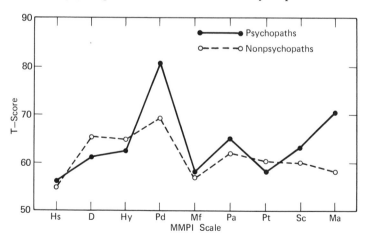

FIGURE 1. Mean MMPI scores for 30 psychopathic and 30 nonpsychopathic criminals (Hare, 1969).

and the Hypomania (*Ma*) scales. The *Pd* scale contains such items as "I am sure I get a raw deal from life" and "I have used alcohol excessively." The *Ma* scale contains such items as "When I get bored I like to stir up some excitement" and "Something exciting will always pull me out of it when I am feeling low."

Individuals with high *Pd* and *Ma* scores are described by Dahlstrom and Welsh (1960).

> Persons with this profile pattern show clear manifestations of psychopathic behavior, the hypomania seemingly energizing or activating the pattern related to . . . [the *Pd* scale]. That is, these people tend to be overactive and impulsive, irresponsible and untrustworthy, shallow and superficial in their relationships. They are characterized by easy morals, readily circumvented consciences, and fluctuating ethical values. To satisfy their own desires and ambitions, they may expend great amounts of energy and effort, but they find it difficult to stick to duties and responsibilities imposed by others. In superficial contacts and social situations they create favorable impressions because of their freedom from inhibiting anxieties and insecurities. They are lively, conversational, fluent, and forthright; they enter wholeheartedly into games, outings, and parties, without being self-conscious or diffident. However, their lack of judgment and control may lead them to excesses of drinking, merrymaking, or teasing. They may be prone to continue activities so long that they exceed the proprieties, neglect other obligations, or alienate others. (p. 192).

Anxiety Scales

Several investigators have used anxiety scales in an attempt to differentiate between psychopathic and neurotic criminals. One of the scales often used is the *Taylor Manifest Anxiety Scale* (MAS). The MAS is a self-report inventory measuring the degree to which an individual admits experiencing manifest symptoms of anxiety (such as "I sweat a great deal"; "My sleep is restless and disturbed").

Van Evra and Rosenberg (1963) used the MAS to divide criminals into low- and high-anxiety groups; the MMPI profiles of the two groups were then compared. The low-anxiety group had higher scores on the *Pd* scale and lower scores on all other scales than did the high-anxiety group. In addition, there was some evidence that the responses of the low-anxiety (psychopathic?) group were more defensive and less indicative of neurotic maladjustment than were those of the high-anxiety (neurotic?) group.

Lykken (1955) found that neurotic criminals had higher MAS scores than did psychopathic criminals or normal noncriminals; the latter two groups did not differ from one another. However, in a more recent study Schoenherr (1964), using similar subjects, was unable to replicate Lykken's findings, although the results were in the same direction as those obtained by Lykken.

Both Lykken and Schoenherr supplemented the MAS with a measure of anxiety derived from the MMPI, the *Anxiety Index*. The results were essentially the same as those obtained with the MAS—Lykken found that neurotic criminals received significantly higher scores than did either of the other two groups, while Schoenherr obtained a similar, though statistically nonsignificant, trend.

Lykken also used a specially constructed scale, the *Activity Preference Questionnaire,* or APQ (described on p. 67), which he felt was more of a measure of anxiety reactivity than was either the MAS or the Anxiety Index. On this scale the psychopaths seemed to be the least, and the normal nonpsychopaths the most anxious.

More recently, Rose (1964) found that psychiatric patients with low scores on the APQ (low anxiety reactivity) had MMPI profiles indicative of psychopathy (irresponsible, immature, demanding, egocentric, impulsive, careless, restless, acting-out). On the other hand, patients with high APQ scores had MMPI profiles indicative of neuroticism (anxious, worried, shy, feelings of inadequacy, fearful, lacking confidence).

The Maudsley Personality Inventory

The *Maudsley Personality Inventory* or *MPI* (Eysenck, 1959) is a self-report inventory designed to measure two dimensions of personality: extraversion and neuroticism. Several investigators have used the MPI to test Eysenck's contention that the psychopath is a neurotic extravert; that is, that he is high on both extraversion and neuroticism (see p. 63).

Contrary to expectation, Schoenherr (1964) found that psychopathic criminals received about the same MPI neuroticism and extraversion scores that neurotic criminals and normal noncriminals received. Moreover, the scores obtained were virtually the same as those generally obtained from normal populations (see Eysenck, 1968, p. 38; Ingham and Robinson, 1964).

Although Berg (1963) found that psychopathic criminals received higher extraversion scores than did neurotic criminals, the mean score received by the psychopaths was about the same as that received by Schoenherr's subjects, and, again, was similar to the scores generally obtained by normal subjects.

Within the framework of Eysenck's theory of personality, therefore, there is no direct evidence that the psychopath is either neurotic or extraverted, at least to the extent that these dimensions are measured by the MPI. However, Eysenck (1964) has suggested that extraversion may be separable into two components—impulsivity and sociability. It is possible that future research will find that psychopaths are high on one component (impulsivity) and not the other.

The Semantic Differential

The *semantic differential* is a procedure developed by Osgood (Osgood, Suci, and Tannenbaum, 1957) for measuring the connotations that an object or concept has. A study by Marks (1965) illustrates its use. The subjects were psychopaths and obsessive-compulsives, representing the high and low ends of a dimension of impulsivity, and a group of orthopedic patients. Each subject was required to rate a series of concepts (for example, "myself," "my father," "my feelings when I am angry," "love," and "fear") on 11 seven-point bipolar adjectives (such as, good-bad, kind-cruel). With this procedure it was possible to compare the three groups of subjects on the connotations that each concept had for them. For example, the profiles plotted in Figure 2 indicate that the three groups differ in their ratings of the concept "my father." Compared with the fathers of the other two groups, the fathers of the psychopaths were more negatively evaluated (more distasteful, dirty, bad, unpleasant, and cruel) and were considered more harmful and dangerous. Similar profiles were obtained for "my mother," findings that are consistent with the evidence of disturbed parent-child relationships in psychopathy and delinquency (discussed in Chapter 7).

The connotative meanings of several other concepts are of interest. The profiles for the concept "myself" suggested that the obsessive-compulsives and the psychopaths had negative self-images, and that the latter saw themselves as being dangerous. This was particularly evident with the concept "my feelings when I am angry"; here, the psychopaths considered themselves to be bad, unpleasant, cruel, excitable, harmful, and dangerous.

The connotations of concepts related to fear and anxiety were about the same for each group, as were most of the concepts having to do with love and affection. The exceptions were interesting. For instance, "sexual intercourse" had negative, dangerous connotations for only one type of subject, female psychopaths. In addition, comparisons of the similarity between various concepts revealed that "love" and "sexual intercourse" had similar connotations for the normal and obsessive-compulsive subjects, but not for the psychopathic ones. For both male and female psychopaths sexual relations appeared to be devoid of love and emotional warmth.

On the basis of these and other findings, Marks suggested that most of the psychopaths feared their aggression and experienced as much anxiety and guilt about their behavior as did the normal subjects. Marks acknowledged, however, that his subjects may have included a large proportion of

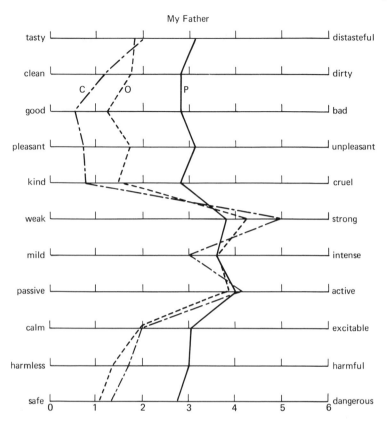

FIGURE 2. Semantic profiles (connotative meanings) of the concept "My father." P = psychopaths; O = obsessive-compulsive; C = normal subjects (after Marks, 1966).

neurotic, anxious criminals, and the results should be considered in this light.[1]

A second study to use the semantic differential technique was carried out by Maas (1966), using female "sociopathic" prisoners with low scores on a self-report inventory of socialization and a normal group consisting of female psychiatric technician trainees. Both groups were matched for age, education, intelligence, and socioeconomic status. Each subject rated eight

---

[1] In Chapter 7 a model of conscience is presented that relates guilt and "resistance to temptation" to punishment techniques. According to this model and the evidence in support of it, guilt feelings for transgressions can coincide with low resistance to temptation, a situation that seems descriptive of the neurotic criminal and the subjects used by Marks. As we shall see, the psychopath has low resistance to temptation and little or no guilt.

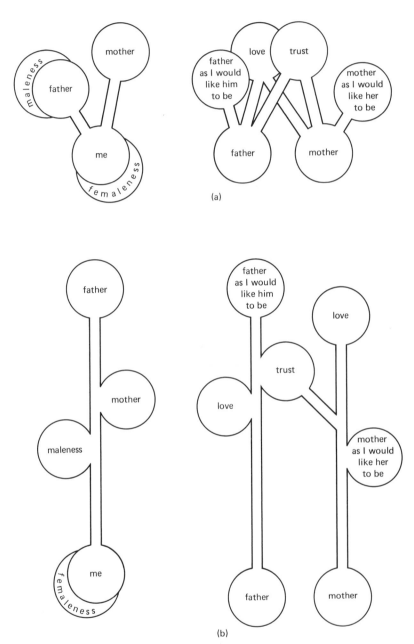

FIGURE 3. Semantic space for (a) normal and (b) sociopathic women (after Maas, 1966).

concepts ("mother," "love," and so forth) on a series of 11 seven-point bipolar adjectives. On the basis of these ratings, it was possible to compare the various concepts in terms of their similarity in meaning. That is, the closer together the concepts were to each other in "semantic space," the more similar they were in meaning. The positions of the concepts in a two-dimensional space are plotted in Figure 3.

The differences between the two groups were quite striking. For the normal subjects, the concepts were close together and their relationships were as we might expect them to be for well-adjusted people. On the other hand, the sociopathic subjects perceived themselves as being very unlike their parents. In addition, the great distance between the parental concepts and "love," "trust," "father as I would like him to be," and "mother as I would like her to be" suggests the existence of disturbed parental relationships and, according to Maas, a failure to identify with parental figures. These findings are similar to those obtained by Marks, although again it is difficult to know what proportion of the subjects were actually psychopaths in the strict sense. Moreover, it would have been useful to have included a group of prisoners with high socialization scores to see whether the results were influenced by being incarcerated.

PROJECTIVE METHODS

In an attempt to tap something more basic than traits revealed by self-report inventories, several investigators have made use of projective tests. In general, a projective test provides a subject with a relatively unstructured or ambiguous stimulus capable of eliciting a variety of responses. Theoretically, the responses elicited are dependent not only on the nature of the stimulus material, but also on the subject's needs, motives, feelings, attitudes, and characteristic modes of adjustment to his environment. Whether projective tests are, in fact, able to tell us anything of real significance about an individual's personality structure has long been a matter of considerable controversy (see review by Fisher, 1967).

The Rorschach Inkblot Test

The *Rorschach Inkblot Test* has been used in several studies of psychopathy. Kingsley (1956), for example, administered the test to psychopathic and nonpsychopathic inmates of a military disciplinary barracks. The responses were scored by two experienced clinical psychologists, and disagreements were resolved by a third psychologist. Compared to the other subjects, significantly more of the psychopathic responses were considered to be indicative of impulsivity, immaturity, hostility, aggressiveness, shallowness, and egocentricity.

Sentence Completion

Kingsley (1956) also had his subjects take the *Sacks Sentence Completion Test,* a semistructured test consisting of a series of sentence stems (for example, "It makes me angry when . . .") that a subject must complete. On the basis of their sentence completions Kingsley concluded that the psychopaths showed greater signs of disturbance in their relationships with authority figures and females than did the nonpsychopaths. However, there were no differences between groups in degree of anxiety and guilt expressed, a finding that led Kingsley to suggest that perhaps he was dealing with neurotic criminals instead of with "true" psychopaths. Similar results were obtained in a later study (Kingsley, 1961) with 25 psychopathic and 25 nonpsychopathic military offenders and 50 nonoffenders. In this study the responses of the psychopaths indicated the presence of *more* guilt feelings than were found in the other two groups. However, further analysis suggested that the guilt feelings of the psychopaths were more indicative of their unpleasant situation than of genuine remorse.

Simon, Holzberg, and Unger (1951) presented psychopathic and normal females with a series of conflict situations in which a choice had to be made between satisfying personal needs and meeting social goals. The conflict situations consisted of two versions of a 40-item sentence-completion test. In one form the items were open-end; that is, the subject could complete the sentence in any way that she wanted. In the other form the subject was presented with the item plus two alternative completions, one representing socially acceptable and the other socially deviant behavior. An example of the type of item used is:

> 27. Mary was going to the movies. Before she came up to the ticket office she noticed that a side door was open, so she . . .
>
> (a) went in.
> (b) notified an usher.

In each case the open-end form was given first and was followed, one week later, by the multiple-choice version.

There were no significant differences between groups in the number of deviant responses given on the multiple-choice version of the test. However, the open-end version revealed marked differences, with the psychopathic group giving more deviant responses than the normal group. One way of interpreting these findings is to assume that when presented with a choice between socially acceptable and more selfish forms of behavior, psychopaths are astute enough to select the former (at least on a verbal level and in the type of hypothetical situation used in the study). However, when not provided with specific clues about the most acceptable thing to do, and when required to fall back on their own judgment, their choice is guided less by social values than by personal needs.

Picture-Frustration Study

Holzberg and Hahn (1952) administered a modification of the *Rosenzweig Picture-Frustration Study* to male psychopathic delinquents and male high school students. The Picture-Frustration Study consists of 24 cartoon-like pictures in which one character is being frustrated. The subject's task is to indicate how this character reacted to his frustration. Responses were scored for type and direction of aggression expressed and for degree of guilt generated by the expression of aggression. Contrary to expectation, the psychopaths were not more punitive than the normal subjects. However, there was some evidence that the expression of aggression elicited less guilt in the psychopaths than in the other subjects.

Thematic Apperception Test

Several studies have used the *Thematic Apperception Test* (*TAT*), which consists of a series of ambiguous pictures about which the subject is required to make up stories—to describe what is going on, what led up to the incident depicted, how the people in the picture feel, and what the outcome will be. The assumption is that the themes reflected in the subject's stories will reveal something about his motives, needs, conflicts, and fantasies.

In one study (Silver, 1963) the TAT was given to psychopathic and nonpsychopathic delinquents, residents of an orphanage, and high school students. Compared to the other subjects, the psychopaths expressed their sexual needs more openly, but showed less achievement striving, guilt feelings, and need for recognition. In addition, their stories tended to be short and indicative of limited fantasy resources, a finding that is consistent with Karpman's (1961) statement that the psychopath's fantasy life is a dull one. One of the functions of fantasy and daydreaming may be to permit an individual to engage in vicarious trial and error in which various courses of action and the possible consequences are run through mentally beforehand (Singer, 1966). It is possible that psychopaths do not have the fantasy resources to do so, which could account for some of their poor judgment, impulsivity, and lack of foresight. It is also possible that whatever fantasy resources they do have are directed toward "exciting" themes instead of toward mental planning (see p. 68).

Some psychoanalytic theories (see Berg, 1963) depict the psychopath as an individual whose antisocial behavior is *ego-syntonic*—that is, is an integral part of his personality and not accompanied by moral apprehension, anxiety, and guilt—and therefore not personally disturbing. In a study with neurotic and psychopathic criminals, Berg (1963) used the TAT to test the hypothesis that the psychopath's sexual and aggressive drives are ego-syntonic and that they are expressed in an impulsive, unsocialized manner. Although the results were in the predicted direction, the difference between groups in "impulse socialization" was not statistically significant. However, there was some indication that the fantasy expression of impulses was more ego-syntonic for the psychopathic than for the neurotic criminals.

Binocular Rivalry

Berg also attempted to investigate impulse socialization at the perceptual (as opposed to the fantasy) level. To do this he used a modification of the prism stereoscope to present pairs of pictures simultaneously. Since the pictures were constructed so as not to "fuse" into a composite picture, binocular rivalry occurred; that is, only one picture could be "seen" at a time. Because each exposure was very brief, the subject had time to perceive only one of the pictures. Six pairs of pictures were used, the members of each pair being roughly comparable in size, outline, and position within the visual field. Each pair of pictures represented some impulse-related theme, such as sex, aggression, or orality. However, the two pictures in any given pair depicted different levels of socialization in the expression of the impulse. In each case one picture represented the direct, socially unacceptable mode of impulse expression, while the other represented a more socialized form of expression. For example, one of the stereograms depicted two men either boxing or brawling, the former representing a more socialized form of physical aggression. Similar pairs of pictures (six pairs altogether) depicted sexual and oral themes. Berg hypothesized that the generally impulsive, unsocialized behavior of the psychopaths would be reflected in a tendency to perceive the less socialized version of each pair. The results supported the hypothesis; the neurotics reported seeing the more socialized picture significantly more often than did the psychopaths.

Some Implications

Taken together with the TAT data, these findings suggest that the overt behavior of the psychopath familiar to clinicians is reflected in a tendency to *perceive* impulsive, unsocialized content. In agreement with Berg's suggestion that the psychopath is able to express his sexual and aggressive drives in a blatant, impulsive way because these drives are ego-syntonic, Van Evra and Rosenberg (1963) have commented, on the basis of responses to a self-report inventory, that ". . . the lack of anxiety and manifest pathology in primary psychopaths may be accounted for on the basis of ego-syntonic deviant behavior and strong inflexible defenses" (p. 63).

These studies do not mean, of course, that the psychopath is unaware of the discrepancy between his behavior and societal expectations, but rather that he is neither guided by the possibility of such a discrepancy nor disturbed by its occurrence. Just why this should be so is not clear, although some possibilities will be discussed in later chapters. For example, it is possible that an inability to acquire conditioned emotional responses makes it difficult for the psychopath to anticipate emotional distress as a result of his actions. Those investigators more psychodynamically disposed may feel that the psychopath is particularly adept at rationalizing his behavior or at using such defense mechanisms as projection and denial. Another possibility, discussed more fully in Chapter 7, is that the psychopath cannot predict how society will react to his behavior because of an inability to role-play, that is, to put himself in another's position. In any case, it is apparent to anyone who has dealt with psychopaths that their behavior and judgment are considerably better on a verbal, intellectual level than in actual practice. This is perhaps most evident when the expression of their needs conflicts with the modes of expression permitted by society.

OTHER PSYCHOMETRIC DEVICES

Porteus Maze

The *Porteus Maze* is a paper-and-pencil test in which the subject is required to trace the correct path through printed mazes of varying difficulty. Performance on this test is assumed to reflect planning capacity, anticipation, and foresight, and has been found to differentiate between delinquents and nondelinquents (see Porteus, 1965). Schalling and Rosén (1968) found that it is also related to ratings of psychopathy; the more psychopathic the subject, the more likely he is to make errors associated with carelessness, poor planning, and disregard for the rules of the test.

Level-of-Aspiration Task

The deviant behavior of the psychopath may also be reflected in his performance on other simple laboratory tasks. For example, Lonstein (1952) used a level-of-aspiration task to test the clinical statements that the psychopath has poor judgment, that he is impulsive and egocentric, and that he lacks insight into his own shortcomings. The subject was required to roll a marble down a groove in such a way that it came to rest in a small depression (target) located midway down the groove and labeled with the number 6. For doing so he received six points. If the marble rolled too far or not far enough, it would come to rest in some other depression; the subject would receive fewer points, depending on how far off the target he was. Before each series of five rolls the subject had to predict how many points he would obtain. If his predicted score (for example, 25) was less than his obtained score (for instance, 27) he was credited with the former. However, if his predicted score (for example, 30) was greater than his obtained score (for instance, 25), he was penalized twice the value of the discrepancy involved; that is, he was credited with only 15 points. Each subject received 11 trials, so that the degree to which his predicted performance (level of aspiration) was influenced by his actual performance could be evaluated. The subjects were all hospitalized veterans, and consisted of psychopaths, neurotics (mostly anxiety reactions), and general medical and surgical cases (normal group). As expected, the level of aspiration shown by the normal subjects was more realistic than that shown by the other groups, in that their predicted and actual scores were similar. The psychopaths, on the other hand, tended to overestimate, and the neurotics to underestimate, how well they would do. The unrealistic level of aspiration shown by the psychopaths is consistent with the clinical impression that they are characterized by an inflated ego and an unrealistic conception of their own abilities (see Thorne, 1959). Also of interest was the reaction shown by the psychopaths to success (actual score equal to or greater than predicted score) and to failure (actual score less than predicted score). Whereas the normal and neurotic subjects lowered their predicted score after a failure, the psychopaths tended to do just the opposite. Lonstein refers to these responses of the psychopaths as "deviant" and sees them as supporting the clinical observation that psychopaths are socially nonconforming individuals.

However, the rationale for this conclusion is not clear. Nor is any evidence presented to suggest that the psychopaths' deviant responses to success and failure are inefficient or maladaptive. For example, given the rules of the task, do the psychopaths obtain lower overall scores as the result of their deviant responses, or do they in fact surpass the other subjects?

SUMMARY

While psychopaths as a group receive at least average scores on global measures of intelligence, more research is needed in which the dimensions of intellect are tapped.

A variety of psychometric devices has been used to study the personality of the psychopath. In general, the results have been reasonably consistent with clinical accounts of psychopathy.

CHAPTER THREE

CORTICAL CORRELATES OF PSYCHOPATHY

Much of the research on psychopathy (and other disorders of behavior—see Stern & McDonald, 1965) is based on the assumption that there is a physiological basis to the disorder. The immediate object of most of this research is to obtain relationships or correlations between physiological (cortical, autonomic) activity and a more overt behavioral aspect of psychopathy. It is important to note, however, that the observation of a relationship between physiological and behavioral events does not necessarily mean that the events are causally related. And even if they are, it is often difficult to specify the direction of the relationship. For instance, it is possible that a cortical disturbance produces some form of abnormal behavior, but it is also possible that the behavior is directly or indirectly responsible for the disturbance. The point is that unless we can manipulate the variables under study experimentally, or unless we have some independent evidence concerning the nature and direction of the relationship involved, we must generally be content with the establishment of physiological correlates of psychopathy. This does not prevent us from using these observed relationships to test hypotheses about the causes of psychopathy and to generate new hypotheses.

Even if we cannot always determine that a physiology-behavior relationship is a causal one, the observation of such a relationship may be important for other reasons. At present, our descriptions of psychopathy are almost entirely clinical in nature. If we could establish that psychopaths differ from other individuals on some physiological variable, this variable might be used as one of the defining characteristics of psychopathy. The resultant combination of clinical and objective criteria would greatly facilitate subsequent research. Moreover, many of the clinical assumptions about psychopathy could be evaluated by making the appropriate physiological observations. For example, the psychopath's presumed absence of anxiety could be tested by taking measurements of autonomic nervous system activity (see Chapter 4) under conditions generally assumed to generate anxiety.

THE ELECTROENCEPHALOGRAM

The electroencephalogram or *EEG* is a recording of the rhythmical and transient fluctuations of the electrical activity of the brain. In the average awake subject the dominant rhythm obtained from the back of the head has a frequency of from 8 to 13 cycles per second (cps) and an amplitude of about 40–50 microvolts (μV). This low-frequency, high-voltage wave is called the *alpha* rhythm (see Figure 4d). Attentiveness, novel visual stimulation, anxiety, and some forms of mental activity generally result in *desynchronization* or *blocking* of the alpha rhythm; that is, it is replaced by a high-frequency (14–25 cps), low-voltage rhythm (the *beta* rhythm) that is more asynchronous than the alpha rhythm. Several low-frequency waves are also found in adult subjects, although excessive amounts in an awake subject are considered abnormal. These slow waves, shown in Figure 4h, are the *theta* (4–7 cps) and the *delta* (less than 4 cps) rhythms. During sleep, the alpha rhythm is gradually replaced by irregular low-voltage activity (Figure 4e), and by an increase in theta and delta activity and 12–14 cps "sleep spindles." In very deep sleep, the EEG consists of generalized high-voltage delta activity with a frequency as low as 1 cps (Figure 4g).

Brain wave activity in infants consists primarily of slow and irregular low-voltage waves. As the child matures, these slow waves are gradually replaced by the faster alpha waves (Figure 4a, b, c). However, in about 10 to 15 percent of the normal population, excessive amounts of slow wave (theta) activity persist into adulthood. A pattern of this type is described as being *immature,* since it is characteristic of the patterns found in children.

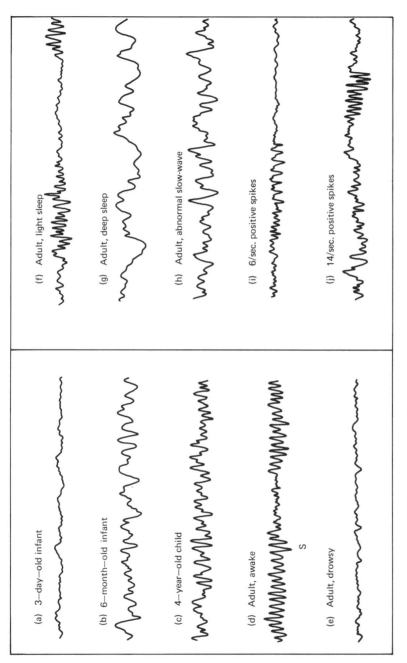

(a) 3—day—old infant

(b) 6—month—old infant

(c) 4—year—old child

(d) Adult, awake

S

(e) Adult, drowsy

(f) Adult, light sleep

(g) Adult, deep sleep

(h) Adult, abnormal slow-wave

(i) 6/sec. positive spikes

(j) 14/sec. positive spikes

FIGURE 4. Some EEG waveforms. The record in (d) shows alpha waves being blocked at point S, and being temporarily replaced by beta waves.

EEG STUDIES OF PSYCHOPATHY

The prolific use of the EEG in the last 25 years has provided a certain amount of ammunition for those who favor a "disease" model of psychopathy. Clinicians have long noted, for example, that certain forms of brain dysfunction are often related to asocial, impulsive, aggressive behavior, and a general lack of behavioral inhibition. Since these behavioral characteristics are also found in psychopaths, many find it difficult to resist concluding that the cause of psychopathy is some type of brain abnormality, resulting, perhaps, from heredity, injury, or disease. After a brief survey of the relevant literature, we shall return to this point.

In a review of mental disorders, Ellingson (1954) reported that 13 out of 14 published studies had found that, in a total of about 1500 psychopaths, between 31 and 58 percent showed some form of EEG abnormality. The most frequent form of abnormality, as the pioneering study by Hill and Watterson (1942) showed, was the presence of slow-wave activity. This slow-wave activity was generally widespread, being present in many parts of the brain.

Many of these studies included a variety of disorders in the classification of "psychopathy." Since we do not know what proportion of subjects were actually psychopathic, it becomes necessary to look at those studies in which somewhat clearer criteria for psychopathy were used. Particularly interesting is the series of studies conducted by Gottlieb and his associates. Their subjects consisted of both adult and adolescent psychopaths. The general characteristics of each group were more or less the same. The results of several studies (Knott, Platt, Ashby, and Gottlieb, 1953) involving over 700 subjects showed remarkable consistency—between 49 and 58 percent of the subjects in each study had EEG abnormalities, generally widespread slow-wave activity. These values closely approximate the incidence of abnormality found in many related studies.

Several other studies are of interest. Ehrlich and Keogh (1956) found that 40 out of 50 psychopathic patients studied had some form of EEG abnormality. A comparison of the behavioral differences between psychopaths with and without EEG abnormalities, however, revealed little of significance. More recently, Arthurs and Cahoon (1963) found that 55 percent of their 87 psychopathic subjects had either borderline or abnormal EEGs. There were no EEG differences between those subjects considered aggressive and those considered passive, but the range of aggressiveness was apparently not very great. Other studies have found that extremely aggressive and dangerous psychopaths are likely to have a higher incidence of EEG abnormality than are those more passive in nature (Ellingson, 1954; Stafford-Clark et al., 1951). The incidence of EEG abnormality found in aggressive psychopaths can apparently be increased and is more easily defined following "activation" by a central nervous system stimulant such as bemegride (Craft, 1965).

Localized Slow-Wave Activity

There is some evidence that extremely impulsive and aggressive psychopaths exhibit EEG abnormalities that are more localized than those discussed in the last section. In a study of severely aggressive psychopaths, Hill (1952) found that about 14 percent (of 194) had abnormal slow-wave activity located in the temporal lobes of the cerebral hemispheres (see Figure 11, p. 61). The incidence of this temporal slow-wave activity in the psychopathic subjects was much higher than that found in normal subjects (2 percent of 146), schizophrenics (4.8 percent of 147), murderers (8.2 percent of 110), and inmates of a prison (2.8 percent of 143). Within the psychopathic group, there was a strong tendency for the incidence of this temporal abnormality to be greater in the highly aggressive than in the less aggressive subjects.

In a more recent study with behavior-problem children, Bay-Rakal (1965) found that the most frequent forms of EEG abnormality included temporal as well as more widespread slow-wave activity. These abnormalities were related to developmental delay, poor control of impulses, poor motor coordination, and inadequate socialization.

Positive Spikes

During the last 20 years a great deal of research has been done on what is often called the *positive-spike* phenomenon (see review by Hughes, 1965). This term refers to bursts of 6–8 cps and 14–16 cps activity, positive in polarity and occurring in the temporal area of the brain (see Figure 4*i, j*). The incidence of positive spikes in the general population is extremely low (1 to 2 percent); however, in severe behavior disorders it may be as high as 20 or 40 percent. The behavior of some patients with positive-spike activity can be quite dramatic (see Schwade and Geiger, 1956, 1960, for some interesting case histories). Typically, the patient has a history of impulsive behavior and overwhelming aggressive and destructive urges. The behavioral act (or "attack") is often precipitated by relatively trivial, innocuous situations, and generally does not stop until its completion. The episode is likely to be extremely unrestrained, violent, and destructive, often resulting in severe damage to property and injury or death to others. In spite of its destructiveness, positive-spike behavior is generally coordinated and well directed and is often performed with considerable skill and precision. Most investigators have observed that at the completion of the act the individual expresses no guilt, anxiety, or remorse for what he has done, and he is often able to discuss it on a verbal level.

Most of the subjects with positive spiking are probably not psychopathic. Nevertheless, the incidence of positive-spike activity among highly impulsive and aggressive psychopaths may be as high as 40 to 45 percent (Kurland, Yeager, & Arthur, 1963).

Implications of EEG Studies

The frequent finding that the brain-wave activity of some psychopaths bears a certain resemblance to that generally found in children has led some investigators to propose that psychopathic behavior reflects cortical immaturity. The simplicity of this *maturational retardation* hypothesis is quite appealing, particularly when it is recognized that some of the psychopath's characteristics—egocentricity, impulsivity, inability to delay gratification—are also found to a certain extent in children.[1]

If psychopathy is related to a slow rate of cortical maturation, we might expect to find that the incidence of psychopathy decreases with age. There is some support for this view. Gibbens, Pond, and Stafford-Clark (1955) note, for example, that psychopaths with EEG abnormalities have a better prognosis than those with normal EEGs; the former presumably outgrow their cortical immaturity. Similarly, Robins (1966) found that about a third of a group of 82 diagnosed psychopaths became less grossly antisocial with age, and that this improvement in behavior occurred most frequently between the ages of 30 and 40. Taken together, it is possible that these findings reflect the delayed but coincident attainment of cortical and social maturation.

The maturational retardation hypothesis has limitations, of course. It does not really explain *why* cortical immaturity produces psychopathy. Nor does it account for the fact that only some aspects of psychopathy bear a resemblance to those of the child. Perhaps the resemblance is only a superficial one; it is unlikely, for example, that the "egocentricity" of the child and the psychopath are really the same thing or that they are related to the same physiological and psychological processes. Moreover, the maturational retardation hypothesis fails to consider the profound effect that environmental experiences are bound to have on the development and

---

[1] Although it is possible that the slow-wave activity on which the hypothesis is based is related to other factors, a recent review by Kiloh and Osselton (1966) concluded that this activity was in fact associated with delayed cerebral maturation. Histologic studies of the nervous system at different age levels lend support to this conclusion. That is, cortical maturation appears to be at least grossly correlated with EEG data (Lindsley, 1964; Scheibel and Scheibel, 1964).

maintenance of psychopathic behavior. Finally, it does not explain why approximately 15 percent of the general population exhibit EEG abnormalities and yet are mentally and behaviorally quite normal. It is possible, of course, that cerebral immaturity *plus* some other organic or environmental factors are required to produce psychopathy. However, these other factors usually are not made clear.

Besides the cortical immaturity hypothesis, the presence of localized EEG abnormalities has led some investigators (for example, Kiloh and Osselton, 1966; MacKay, 1965) to suggest that psychopathy is related to some type of structural or functional disorder within the brain. This possibility, though plausible, must be tempered by the knowledge that an EEG abnormality does not necessarily mean that there is a corresponding brain abnormality; nor, for that matter, does a normal EEG always indicate the absence of a brain disorder (Kiloh and Osselton, 1966).

This of course does not mean that the observation of EEG abnormalities cannot be used as the basis for developing hypotheses about the cortical functioning of psychopathic persons. Consider, for example, the following line of reasoning which, though highly speculative, is consistent with the EEG findings already reported and also with recent research with experimentally induced brain lesions.

We have already noted that besides widespread slow-wave activity, the EEG records of some psychopaths, especially the highly aggressive and explosively impulsive ones, contain evidence of slow-wave and positive-spike activity apparently emanating from the temporal lobes and the associated limbic system. It is quite possible, as some investigators have suggested, that these EEG abnormalities reflect some sort of dysfunction in the underlying temporal and limbic mechanisms. Although these mechanisms are complex and their functions not yet well understood, it is known that they are involved in sensory and memory processes and in the central regulation of emotional and motivational behavior. For our purposes, it is sufficient to note that the limbic system appears to have both facilitatory and inhibitory effects on behavior; that is, activity in some mechanisms facilitates and maintains ongoing behavior; activity in other mechanisms inhibits or disrupts ongoing behavior (see Grossman, 1967; McCleary, 1966). These limbic mechanisms appear to play a particularly important role in the regulation of fear-motivated behavior, including learning to inhibit a response in order to avoid punishment (*passive-avoidance* learning). Research reviewed by McCleary (1966), for instance, indicates that lesions in the limbic inhibitory mechanisms make it difficult to learn to inhibit a punished response. A more general effect of these lesions may be to produce *perseveration* of the most dominant response in a given situation. That is, the response with the greatest tendency to occur (either because of some inherent tendency or because of past learning experiences) will occur, even though it had previously been inhibited because of punishment.

On the basis of this research, we might hypothesize that the temporal slow-wave activity frequently observed in the EEG records of psychopaths reflects a malfunction of some limbic inhibitory mechanism and that this malfunction makes it difficult to learn to inhibit behavior that is likely to lead to punishment.[2] This malfunction could result from hereditary or experiential factors or, more likely, from injury, disease, or biochemical or vascular changes that temporarily dampen the inhibiting activity of important mechanisms. According to McCleary's concept of response perseveration, the result would be that the most dominant response in any given situation would tend to occur regardless of its consequences. For example, the tendency to engage in some form of sexual behavior generally increases when sexual drives are high (because of prolonged sexual deprivation, the presence of sex-related cues, and so forth). The actual form that sexual behavior takes depends on such things as learning and the nature of the opportunities available. But even though response tendencies of a sexual kind are dominant, they may be inhibited because of social restrictions, unwillingness of the intended partner, fear of pregnancy, disease, or sexual inadequacy. If we assume that the effectiveness of such restrictions is dependent on the normal functioning of limbic inhibitory mechanisms, and if we further assume that under certain conditions these mechanisms malfunction in the psychopath, we would then predict that, given the urge, he would initiate and complete the act despite the restrictions. The clinical comments that the psychopath's behavior is impulsive and determined more by his immediate needs than by possible consequences could thus be interpreted in terms of the failure of the appropriate inhibitory mechanisms to function properly.

Cortical Excitability

Stimulation of a sensory receptor sets up a neural impulse that "travels" along various pathways to the appropriate cortical area. If electrodes are placed on the scalp over this cortical area, the impulse or *evoked potential* can be picked up and recorded. When the sensory receptor is stimulated twice in rapid succession, the size of the second evoked potential reflects the extent to which the neural system involved has recovered from the effects of the first stimulus. By varying the interval between successive stimuli and observing the resulting effect on the magnitude of the second

---

[2] Douglas (1967), in a recent review, suggested that slow-wave activity is associated with a reduction in the inhibitory function of one of the limbic areas, the hippocampus.

evoked potential, it is possible to determine the rate at which neural recovery occurs.

Shagass and Schwartz (1962) found that the rate of recovery from the effects of stimulation of the ulnar nerve (at the wrist) was related to psychiatric diagnosis. Briefly, both normal and neurotic subjects recovered more quickly than did schizophrenics and psychopaths. The fact that the latter two groups recovered at about the same rate was interpreted by Shagass and Schwartz as support for the view that psychopathy is more closely related to psychosis than to neurosis.

In interpreting their findings, Shagass and Schwartz have considered and rejected the hypotheses that slow cortical recovery reflects brain damage or that it is associated with EEG abnormalities of the type discussed earlier. In this regard, their conclusion that psychopathy and psychosis are related needs closer examination, since psychopaths show evidence of slow cortical recovery *plus* abnormal EEGS, while psychotics apparently exhibit only slow recovery. An alternative hypothesis, and one with empirical support, is that recovery rate is a reflection of *cortical excitability*—the faster the rate of recovery, the greater the degree of cortical excitability (Harter, 1967). The psychopaths' slow recovery rate would therefore imply that they are characterized by a reduced state of cortical excitability, a possibility considered at length in Chapter 5. For the present, it is worth noting that in a recent neuropsychological model of emotion (Pribram, 1967), reduced states of cortical excitability are considered to be the result of cortical inhibitory mechanisms that influence the rate with which cells in the brain recover their excitability. Pribram further suggested that these inhibitory mechanisms [3] may underlie such processes as repression, suppression, and perceptual defense, since each appears to be a form of defensive "gating out" of stimuli that initiate disturbing emotional states. With reference to psychopathy, therefore, we might hypothesize that the disorder is related to the operation of inhibitory defensive mechanisms that exert control over sensory input that would ordinarily have disturbing consequences. This topic is also taken up on page 69.

SUMMARY

In spite of their limitations, the EEG studies of psychopathy have produced rather consistent results. One finding, that the widespread slow-wave activity often found in psychopaths bears a certain resemblance to the

[3] It should be noted that inhibitory mechanisms that regulate sensory input are not the same as the inhibitory mechanisms related to the control of behavior.

EEG patterns usually found in children, has led to a *cortical immaturity* hypothesis of psychopathy. A second hypothesis, based on the presence of localized EEG abnormalities, is that psychopathy is associated with a defect or malfunction of certain brain mechanisms concerned with emotional activity and the regulation of behavior. Finally, it has been suggested that psychopathy may be related to a lowered state of cortical excitability and to the attenuation of sensory input, particularly input that would ordinarily have disturbing consequences.

CHAPTER FOUR

AUTONOMIC CORRELATES OF PSYCHOPATHY

In the last chapter we discussed the hypothesis, held by biologically oriented investigators, that psychopathy is associated with some form of brain dysfunction, possibly in the limbic and related systems. Other investigators have attempted to relate psychopathy to the functioning of the autonomic nervous system. The majority of these investigators has relied on one or more of the following assumptions: (1) that a complete description of psychopathy must involve physiological variables; (2) that many of the psychopath's characteristics—his apparent lack of anxiety, guilt, or remorse, his inability to empathize with others, his shallow emotional involvements, his failure to be influenced by threatened punishment—have autonomic components; and (3) that studies of autonomic activity provide a basis for testing predictions derived from theories of psychopathy.

THE AUTONOMIC NERVOUS SYSTEM

Space limitations permit only a very brief description of the autonomic nervous system (ANS). More detailed presentations have been made by Grossman (1967) and Sternbach (1966).

The nervous system can be subdivided on the basis of either structure or function. Division on a structural basis yields two main systems: the

37

central nervous system (CNS), which includes the brain, brain stem, and the spinal cord; and the *peripheral nervous system* (PNS), which includes everything outside of the CNS. According to this scheme, the ANS is primarily peripheral, although some of its nerve fibers originate and terminate within the CNS. Division on the basis of function also yields two main systems: the *somatic,* consisting of the CNS and the nerve fibers running to and from the striated muscles and the sensory organs; and the *visceral,* consisting of the nerves that activate the visceral organs, including the stomach, intestines, glands, heart, lungs, and so on. The visceral system is also called the *autonomic nervous system.*

The ANS itself can be subdivided on the basis of either structure or function. Structural subdivision (see Figure 5) results in two main systems: *the sympathetic nervous system* (SNS), consisting of nerve fibers that leave

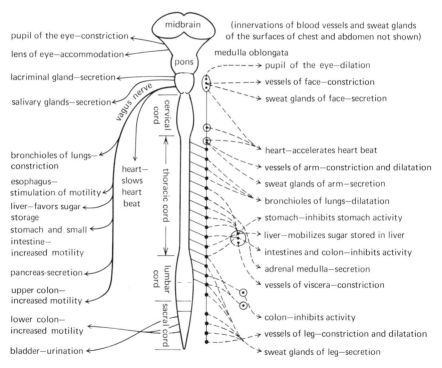

FIGURE 5. **The structure and functions of the sympathetic and the parasympathetic divisions of the autonomic nervous system. Only half of each division is shown here. Both divisions send fibers to both sides of the body (from Ruch, 1963).**

the spinal cord in the thoracic and lumbar regions; and the *parasympathetic nervous system* (PNS), consisting of nerves emerging from the cranial and sacral regions of the CNS. Each of the nerves of the ANS has a junction or synapse in a ganglion (group of nerve cells) between the CNS and the organ it innervates. The fibers entering the ganglia are called *preganglionic* and those leaving the ganglia are called *postganglionic*. The preganglionic fibers in the sympathetic division are generally short and connect to many ganglia; the result is that the activity of the sympathetic division is diffuse, with many organs being simultaneously innervated. Unlike the SNS, the PNS has long preganglionic fibers, with the synapse near the end organ. The result is that the activity of this system is relatively specific.

The autonomic system can also be subdivided, on a functional basis, into *adrenergic* and *cholinergic* systems. When a nerve impulse reaches a synapse, a chemical substance is released that stimulates the next nerve. The substance secreted by both the sympathetic and the parasympathetic preganglionic fibers is *acetylcholine* (ACH). The postganglionic fibers of the PNS also stimulate their respective end organs with acetylcholine. However, most of the postganglionic fibers of the SNS stimulate their end organs by releasing a substance similar to *noradrenalin*. Generally speaking, this division of the ANS into the adrenergic (noradrenalin) and cholinergic (ACH) systems corresponds to the structural division into SNS and PNS. However, there are exceptions. For example, the sweat glands are activated by SNS fibers, but the postganglionic fibers in this case release acetylcholine; that is, they are cholinergic. The adrenal glands are also innervated by preganglionic SNS fibers which, of course, release acetylcholine.

The effects that sympathetic and parasympathetic innervation have on the various end organs are summarized in Table 2. In most cases, an organ receives innervation from both SNS and PNS fibers. As seen in Table 2, the effects of these fibers are generally (though not always) antagonistic, so that equilibrium is maintained in the bodily functions. Several end organs, however, receive only SNS fibers. These include the sweat glands, hair follicles, and the peripheral blood vessels.

Besides maintaining equilibrium in bodily functioning, the ANS plays an important role in emotional behavior. In general, the SNS is dominant during periods of stress and emotional arousal; increases occur in blood pressure, heart rate, respiration rate, and so on. The PNS is usually dominant during periods of relative quiescence.

Two other functions of the ANS are relevant here. These are its influence on level of cortical arousal, and its relationship to attentiveness and sensitivity to environmental stimulation. Both functions are discussed later.

TABLE 2: Effects of Sympathetic and Parasympathetic Activity on Various Organs

Organ	Sympathetic Effect	Parasympathetic Effect
Heart	Acceleration	Deceleration
Peripheral blood vessels	Constriction	None
Sweat glands	Secretion	None
Pupil	Dilation	Constriction
Adrenal glands	Secretion	None
Salivary glands	Secretion (?)	Secretion
Lungs (bronchia)	Dilation	Constriction
Pilomotor cells	Piloerection	None
Gastro-intestinal tract	Inhibition of peristalsis	Peristalsis
Genitalia	Ejaculation	Erection

RESTING LEVELS OF AUTONOMIC ACTIVITY

Does the psychopath differ from others in the way in which his ANS functions when he is in a relatively quiescent or resting state? It is difficult to provide a firm answer to this question for several reasons: the number of relevant studies is very small; somewhat differing criteria for psychopathy and different testing and recording procedures have been used; most investigators have restricted their recording to one index of autonomic activity instead of obtaining simultaneous recordings of a number of autonomic variables; and no studies have looked at psychopaths under conditions that could truly be called "resting" or quiescent. Since the experimental situation itself functions as a complex stimulus, we have no way of knowing to what extent observed autonomic activity involves a *response* to the experimental situation. The problem is complicated by the fact that the experimental situation and its significance to the subjects differs from study to study. When we speak of a resting state, therefore, it should be clear that the term is used only in a relative sense to refer to level of autonomic activity observed in a given experimental situation. In most studies, the subjects are simply lying or sitting quietly.

Early studies by Lindner (1942) and by Ruilmann and Gulo (1950) found that groups of psychopathic criminals and either criminal or noncriminal control groups did not differ appreciably in resting levels of skin resistance, heart rate, respiration rate, and blood pressure. Both of these studies had methodological limitations that made them difficult to assess; however, a recent, more sophisticated study by Goldstein (1965) obtained similar results. Although the psychopaths in Goldstein's study had a slightly lower level of skin conductance and slightly higher respiration and heart rates than a nonpatient group, the differences were not significant. There were also no systematic differences between the two groups in resting muscle tension.

Although each of these studies obtained multiple measures of autonomic activity, it is possible that the failure to find any differences between groups was due to the use of relatively heterogeneous groups of subjects. In a recent study (Hare, 1968a), those inmates of a federal penitentiary who clearly met Cleckley's criteria of psychopathy (see p. 5) were classified as psychopaths. Inmates who met many of the criteria but about whom there was some doubt constituted a mixed group. The remaining inmates had relatively few psychopathic features. The first part of the experiment (the rest is discussed on pp. 44–48) was used to obtain resting measures of autonomic activity; in each case the measures were taken after the subject had been sitting quietly in a semireclining position for about 15 minutes. The results are presented in Table 3. The differences between groups in respiratory activity were small and not statistically significant. However, both measures of palmar electrodermal activity tended to differentiate between groups. The psychopathic and mixed groups had signifi-

TABLE 3: Mean Resting Levels of Autonomic Functioning in Psychopathic and Nonpsychopathic Criminals (After Hare, 1968a.)

Variable	Group		
	Psychopaths (N = 21)	Mixed Group (N = 18)	Nonpsychopaths (N = 12)
Palmar electrodermal activity			
Log skin conductance / cm²	1.2	1.2	1.4
Nonspecific GSRs / min	3.4	3.9	5.5
Cardiac activity			
Heart rate	78.8	73.6	75.4
Heart rate variability	7.9	7.8	9.6
Respiratory activity			
Respiration rate	15.8	15.9	15.0
Regularity [a]	1.5	1.8	1.4
I-fraction [b]	0.4	0.4	0.4

[a] Scored on a 3-point scale, with 1 being most regular.
[b] Proportion of total respiratory cycle given to inspiration.

cantly lower levels of resting skin conductance [1] than did the nonpsychopathic group. More or less identical results have been obtained in two earlier studies in which psychopaths were compared with both criminal and noncriminal control groups (Hare, 1965a, 1965b). Although these differences in skin conductance may be due to structural factors such as the number and distribution of sweat glands in the palms, it is also possible that they reflect a lower resting state of sympathetic arousal in psychopaths.

The other index of electrodermal activity consisted of the frequency with which nonspecific galvanic skin responses (GSRs) occurred. These are transient increases in skin conductance that occur in the absence of any specific eliciting stimuli. Inspection of Table 3 indicates that the least amount of nonspecific GSR activity was obtained among the psychopaths, although the differences between groups were not quite statistically significant. Similar results have been obtained in two other experiments. In one study (Fox & Lippert, 1963), psychopaths exhibited significantly less resting nonspecific GSR activity than did nonpsychopaths, while in the other study (Lippert & Senter, 1966) there was also less activity among the psychopaths but the difference was not significant. Taken together then, the consistency of these studies suggests that psychopaths tend to be characterized by a somewhat lower level of nonspecific GSR activity than that found in nonpsychopaths. Since this index of electrodermal activity, like skin conductance, appears to be positively related to the degree of sympathetic arousal, we might take this to be further evidence that psychopaths are sympathetically underaroused while in a state of relative quiescence.

As Table 3 indicates, the resting heart rate of the psychopaths was slightly greater than that of the other groups. Although the differences were small and not statistically significant, it is interesting that a similar trend has been reported in at least two other studies (Goldstein, 1965; Schachter and Latané, 1964). On the surface, such findings appear to conflict with the inference (based on electrodermal data) that the psychopath at rest is in a low state of sympathetic arousal. If that inference is correct, should we not also find that the psychopath has a comparatively slow heart rate (since sympathetic activity produces cardiac acceleration)? However, several considerations indicate that the conflict may be more apparent than real. First, cardiac activity, unlike electrodermal activity, is regulated by both the sympathetic and parasympathetic divisions of the autonomic nervous system. It is possible, therefore, that any decrement in the activity of the psychopath's sympathetic cardiac accelerators is offset by a similar dec-

---

[1] Because of certain assumptions about the nature of sweat gland activity, skin resistance is often converted to its reciprocal, conductance.

rement in parasympathetic restraint, with the result that his heart rate is normal. Second, it is well known that the correlations between the various indices of autonomic activity are generally quite small. For example, subjects with a high level of skin conductance do not necessarily have high heart rates.[2]

The other index of cardiac activity listed in Table 3 is heart rate fluctuation or variability, defined as the average size of the fluctuations in heart rate that occur from moment to moment. It is evident that the heart rate of the psychopaths was somewhat less variable than that of the nonpsychopathic subjects, although the difference was not significant.

Since nonspecific GSR activity and fluctuations in heart rate both involve variability within an autonomic system, they were combined in a multivariate analysis (Morrison, 1967) to provide a composite index of *autonomic variability*. The result was that the psychopaths exhibited significantly less autonomic variability than did the nonpsychopaths, with the mixed group falling in between. This finding, along with the earlier comments about heart rate, has some interesting implications concerning autonomic-cortical coupling and the regulation of sensory input by the psychopath. Discussion of these implications will be deferred until later.

AUTONOMIC RESPONSIVITY

The psychopath is often described as an individual who lacks the ability to respond emotionally to situations that most people find either stressful or of some interpersonal significance. Cleckley (1964), for example, stated:

> Regularly we find in him extraordinary poise rather than jitteriness or worry, a smooth sense of physical well being instead of uneasy preoccupation with bodily functions. Even under concrete circumstances that would for the ordinary person cause embarrassment, confusion, acute insecurity, or visible agitation, his relative serenity is likely to be noteworthy (p. 267).

Similarly, Karpman (1961) suggested that psychopaths are physiologically unresponsive in situations ordinarily considered to be emotional in nature. In effect, the physiological (autonomic) correlates of emotional experience are assumed to be either absent or at least severely reduced.

---

[2] There are several reasons for this, including what have been called the principles of *situational specificity* and *individual-response stereotypy* (see Sternbach, 1966, for a very readable account of these concepts). Briefly, situational specificity means that the pattern of autonomic activity is dependent on the characteristics of the situation as perceived by the subject. Individual-response stereotypy means that individuals respond to a variety of stimulus situations with what is for them a characteristic and idiosyncratic pattern of autonomic activity.

A related assumption is that the psychopath discharges his tensions readily. Typical of this view is Karpman's (1961) statement:

> Because the psychopath has no conflicts within and lacks long term goals, there is no accumulation of tension as there is in the neurotic. Tension rises quickly in the psychopath in response to instinctive urges, tension which is immediate in nature and which demands immediate release (p. 607).

Karpman further stated that whatever psychological tensions the psychopath does have are devoid of visceral (autonomic) overtones.

All of this suggests that the psychopath should be autonomically underresponsive in situations usually considered to have some emotional significance. Before discussing the research pertinent to this suggestion, however, some data concerning autonomic responsivity to simple stimuli and relatively nonemotional situations will be considered.

Autonomic Responsivity to Simple Stimuli

Ruilmann and Gulo (1950) reported that a group of 18 psychopaths gave smaller galvanic skin responses (GSRs) to "somatic sensory stimuli" than did a group of 47 hospital personnel of similar age and sex distribution. There were no differences in heart rate, respiration rate, or blood pressure responses. Unfortunately, the stimuli used were not identified, nor were any quantitative data (beyond several graphs) provided. In a more recent study, Lippert and Senter (1966) presented 21 psychopathic and 21 nonpsychopathic adolescent inmates of a detention unit with a random series of strong visual and auditory stimuli. There were no differences between groups in the mean magnitude of the GSRs elicited by these stimuli. An additional measure of electrodermal responsivity was the increase that stimulation produced in the frequency of nonspecific GSRs. Again, there were no appreciable differences between groups.

Both of these studies used heterogeneous groups of psychopaths. Further, the former study had methodological limitations and the latter was confined to only one autonomic variable, electrodermal activity. For details on what happens when more clearly defined psychopaths and multiple recordings are used, we can consider a recent study (Hare, 1968a) already referred to in the section on resting ANS activity (p. 41).

After a resting period, subjects heard a series of 15 identical tones. Then they were presented with a sixteenth tone, lower in frequency and intensity than the preceding 15. The mean change in skin conductance (GSR) shown by each group to the 15 repetitive tones and to the novel sixteenth tone is plotted in Figure 6. Statistical analysis indicated that there were no significant differences between groups, either in the magnitude of GSR elicited by the tones or in the rate at which response magni-

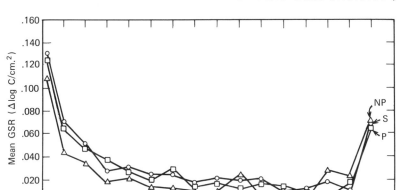

FIGURE 6. Mean GSR to repetitive stimulation (tones 1–15) and to novel stimulation (tone 16). P = psychopaths; S = mixed group; NP = nonpsychopaths (from Hare, 1968a).

tude decreased (habituated) with repeated stimulation. Since the curves plotted in Figure 6 are almost identical with those generally obtained from normal subjects under comparable conditions, we can conclude that psychopaths are quite normal on at least this index of sympathetic responsivity. The mean digital vasoconstriction (contraction of the blood vessels of the fingers) to each of the tones is plotted in Figure 7. As was the case with the GSR, the differences between groups, both in response magnitude and in rate of habituation, were small and not significant. The exceptions were the gradual increase in response magnitude shown by psychopaths

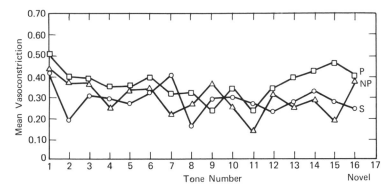

FIGURE 7. Mean digital vasoconstriction to repetitive stimulation (tones 1–15) and to novel stimulation (tone 16). P = psychopaths; S = mixed group; NP = nonpsychopaths (from Hare, 1968a).

during tones 11 to 15, and the comparatively small responses given by the psychopathic and mixed groups to the novel sixteenth tone.

When cardiac responsivity is considered, differences between groups are more apparent. Figure 8 shows the mean beat-by-beat heart rate changes given by each group to the first tone. Heart rate is plotted for the five beats preceding the onset of tone and for the 20 beats immediately following. It is evident that following tone onset the response was primarily one of marked deceleration for all three groups. The mean deceleration shown by the psycopaths, mixed group, and nonpsychopaths was 4.2, 4.7, and 6.3 beats per minute, respectively.

Figure 9 illustrates the effect that repetitive presentation of the same tone had on the cardiac decelerative response. We have already mentioned the responses given to the first tone. After this initial response, the magnitude of cardiac deceleration gradually decreased (habituated). The rate of decrease was less for the psychopaths than for the other subjects. Perhaps

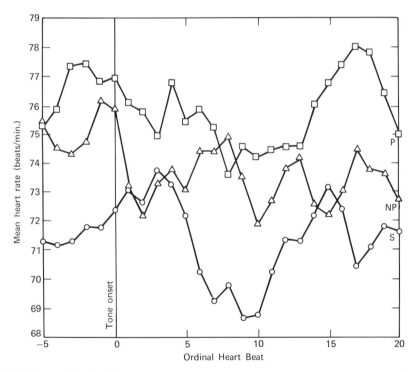

FIGURE 8. Beat-by-beat heart rate in response to tone 1. *P* = psychopaths; *S* = mixed group; *NP* = nonpsychopaths (after Hare, 1968a).

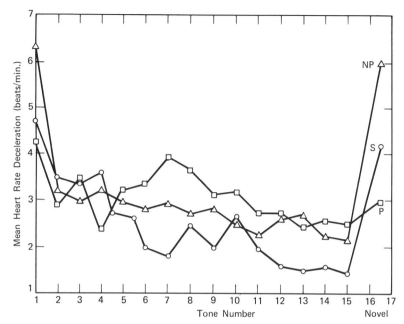

FIGURE 9. **Mean heart rate deceleration to repetitive stimulation (tones 1–15) and to novel stimulation (tone 16). P = psychopaths; S = mixed group; NP = nonpsychopaths (from Hare, 1968a).**

more interesting was the finding that presentation of the novel sixteenth tone resulted in the reappearance of the previously habituated response for all but the psychopaths. The small response given by the psychopaths seems particularly odd when it is realized that their GSR to the novel tone was similar in magnitude to that given by the other subjects.

The results of this study can be interpreted in several ways. One interpretation is based on the Russian conception of the *orienting response* (Sokolov, 1963; see also the recent review by Lynn, 1966). The orienting response (OR) is a nonspecific, complex response to changes in stimulation. It involves turning the body or sensory receptors toward the source of stimulation, blocking of the EEG alpha rhythm, contraction of the blood vessels in the fingers (digital vasoconstriction), dilation of the blood vessels in the head (cephalic vasodilation), increase in skin conductance, pupil dilation, cardiac deceleration, inhibition of respiration, and an increase in muscle tension. One effect of the OR is to increase an organism's sensitivity to novel or unfamiliar stimulation. If the stimulus is a repetitive one, without signal value for the subject, the OR habituates, but returns when a novel stimulus is presented. Western investigators have recently become greatly interested in the OR, and have confirmed many of the Russian findings.[3]

Referring back to Figure 9, we can see that the cardiac component of the OR to novel stimulation (tones 1 and 16) was considerably smaller in the psychopaths than in the nonpsychopaths. One tentative conclusion would be that the psychopath is somewhat less attentive and sensitive to changes in environmental stimulation than is the normal individual. Much the same possibility, based on assumptions about the psychopath's lowered state of cortical excitability, was raised in the last chapter.

A somewhat similar interpretation is suggested by the results of a study by McDonald, Johnson, and Hord (1964). These investigators presented normal subjects with a series of repetitive tones and observed the rate at which various components of the OR habituated. They found that when their subjects were divided, on the basis of EEG criteria, into those who showed signs of drowsiness during the experiment and those who did not (refer to Figure 4), different habituation patterns emerged. Briefly, the GSR, cardiac, and vasomotor responses of their drowsy and alert subjects were remarkably similar, respectively, to those of the psychopaths and the nonpsychopaths in the Hare (1968a) study described above. It is possible, therefore, that the psychopaths in the latter study exhibited a pattern of autonomic responses characteristic of drowsy, cortically under-aroused subjects. The results of a study by Forssman and Frey (1953) are consistent with this possibility. These investigators found a greater incidence of slow-wave activity in psychopathic boys than in a comparable group of normal boys. In addition, the psychopathic boys tended to fall asleep more readily during the EEG examination. On the basis of these findings, Forssman and Frey suggested that a wavering or decrease in attentiveness is characteristic of the psychopathic personality. In commenting on this study, Stern and McDonald (1965) raised the additional possibility that the tendency of psychopaths to become drowsy in experimental situations may reflect the fact these situations generate less stress or anxiety in them than is the case with normal subjects.

Autonomic Responsivity During Stress

Compared to the often severe psychological and physical stresses encountered in everyday life, those involved in most studies of psychopathy must be considered very mild. Although our understanding of psychopathy would no doubt benefit greatly from the use of a variety of more severe

---

[3] All novel stimuli do not produce the OR in the form just described. If the stimulus is noxious or very intense, a *defensive reflex* (DR) may be elicited. The components of the DR include an increase in skin conductance, cardiac acceleration, and both digital and cephalic vasoconstriction.

and more realistic stressful situations, particularly those involving interpersonal behavior, these benefits must be balanced against ethical and moral considerations. Consider, for example, a study by Milgram (1963), in which naive subjects were ordered to administer increasingly severe shocks to a victim supposedly involved in a learning experiment (the victim was actually a stooge who received no shocks). The surprising factor about this experiment was that in spite of extreme personal distress, the naive subjects continued to increase the intensity of the shock that they believed was being delivered to their victim. One would think that empathy and compassion for their supposed victim would induce these subjects to discontinue the administration of shock, but in many cases they did not. Needless to say, it would be most interesting to observe a psychopath's reactions to such a situation. Although Milgram did not record physiological processes, we can be certain that the extreme distress associated with hurting the victim was accompanied by a considerable amount of autonomic activity. Would the psychopath also show distress? Most clinicians say that he is callous and not really concerned about others, although, as Cleckley pointed out, he can *mimic* the appropriate emotions. We might, therefore, expect that a psychopath would verbally express concern while increasing the intensity of the shock he felt someone else was receiving, but at the same time his verbalizations would not be accompanied by the appropriate autonomic components.[4] Since studies of this type have not as yet been done, we must be content with those that have used relatively mild stress.

Lie Detection Situations

The psychopath is generally considered to be a "pathological liar," and we might therefore expect him to behave differently in a lie detection situation than would nonpsychopaths. As part of a larger study, Lykken (1955) required psychopathic criminals, a mixed group of criminals (probably consisting of neurotics and misclassified psychopaths), and a noncriminal, nonpsychopathic control group to choose a number between 1 and 5 and then to conceal the number chosen by replying "no" each time they were asked "Was it—?" The mixed group of criminals gave significantly larger GSRs to the "correct" number (that is, the number "lied" about)

---

[4] Ax (1962) has suggested that empathy and the accurate perception of another's feelings and attitudes may require the construction of an "emotional facsimile" involving the higher centers of the autonomic nervous system. If these centers are preoccupied with other processes, such as hostility or emotional activity concerned with the self, or if they do not function properly, they may be unable to create the "empathic hypotheses" needed to simulate another's feelings. The implication here is that the psychopath's lack of empathy may be associated with an inability to give the appropriate autonomic responses to the suffering and distress of others and to situations involving the interpersonal exchange of love, affection, cruelty, and so forth.

than did the nonpsychopaths. The responses of the psychopaths fell in between these two groups but did not differ significantly from them. More interesting, however, was the ratio between the responses to the "correct" number and the mean of the four "incorrect" numbers: mean GSR to the correct number, divided by mean GSR to the incorrect numbers. The largest "lie-ratio" was obtained by the nonpsychopaths and the smallest by the psychopaths. This simply means that the nonpsychopaths gave considerably larger responses to the "correct" number than to the incorrect ones, while the psychopaths gave about the same magnitude of response to all numbers. This is, of course what we would expect if a psychopath is less disturbed by lying than is a normal person—the autonomic correlates of lying are for the psychopath no different from those of telling the truth. However, we must be cautious about concluding too much from these results; as Lykken and others (Hare, 1968a) have noted, the psychopath is likely to view experimental situations as more of a challenge than a threat. Lykken, for example, suggested that his psychopaths might have been "challenged by the lie detector and motivated to 'beat' the device as a matter of pride, therefore showing a mild degree of (nonanxious) excitement throughout this part of the experiment (p. 173)." He reported further that one psychopath revealed after testing that he had "beat" the test by digging one thumbnail under the other to produce responses to the "wrong" numbers.

Although it did not involve psychopathic subjects, a study by Block (1957) is relevant here. Male medical school applicants were put into a lie detection situation similar to that used by Lykken, and in addition received personality assessments from five psychologists. On the basis of their GSR reactivity to the lie detection situation, the subjects were classified into two groups, Reactors and Nonreactors. From an examination of the psychological assessments it appears that the Reactors were somewhat similar to anxious neurotics while the Nonreactors bore some resemblance to psychopaths. Regarding these (and other) findings, Block suggested:

> Some individuals experience too much affect, e.g., anxiety neurotics, and are thereby incapacitated. But others do not experience sufficient emotion, and therefore do not react on the basis of an implicit but culturally shared set of behavioral premises. Because they operate from a different premise system, these individuals are more likely to emit behavior which is inconceivable to the affectively responsive observer. Such people include the primary psychopath . . . (p. 15).

Both of these lie detection situations are, of course, highly artificial. It would be extremely interesting, therefore, if some means were found whereby the autonomic activity of psychopaths could be monitored in more realistic situations. For example, it should be possible to use the recent advances in telemetry (see Wolff, 1967) to observe autonomic activity during interviews and social interaction without the subject feeling that he is part of an experiment.

Noxious Stimuli

Several studies have investigated the psychopath's responsivity to physical stress, generally electric shock. An early study by Lindner (1942) found that psychopaths did not differ from normal subjects in the magnitude of cardiac, respiratory, and galvanic skin responses to "disturbing" tones and electric shock. More recently, two studies by Hare (1965b, 1965c) found that psychopaths did not differ from normal subjects in the magnitude of GSR elicited by painful electric shock. Goldstein (1965) used white noise instead of shock, and found that a group of psychopaths did not differ from a normal control group in the magnitude of GSR, cardiac, respiratory, blood pressure or muscle tension responses elicited. However, different results were obtained by Lykken (1955). In a classical conditioning paradigm (see Chapter 5), he found that psychopaths gave significantly smaller GSRs to shock than did nonpsychopathic subjects.

With the exception of Goldstein's investigation, all of the studies just mentioned involved designs in which the shock followed some sort of warning signal; that is, they were either classical conditioning paradigms or something similar. The learning or conditioning involved in these studies will be discussed in a later chapter. For the present, however, the fact that shock was preceded by a warning signal makes it difficult to draw any conclusions about the psychopath's reactivity to shock per se. Kimmel (1966) has recently reviewed evidence suggesting that the response (for example, GSR) elicited by a noxious stimulus is smaller when the noxious stimulus is preceded by a warning signal than when it is presented alone. There are probably individual differences in the extent to which warning signals are able to inhibit responses to noxious stimuli (see Lykken, 1968). As we shall see later, it is possible that the inhibitory effects of such signals may be greater for psychopaths than for nonpsychopaths. This would mean that in most of the studies just presented, autonomic reactivity to shock was probably reduced by the inhibitory influence of the warning signals used. Obviously, more research is needed in which noxious stimuli are presented both with and without warning signals.

INDIVIDUAL DIFFERENCES IN RANGE OF AUTONOMIC ACTIVITY

Before proceeding further, we should consider the suggestion (Lykken, 1968) that comparisons of autonomic activity may be more meaningful when individual differences in the *range* of activity possible are taken into account. Assume, for example, that individual *A* responds to a noxious stimulus with a 10-beats-per-minute increase in heart rate, while individual *B* responds to the same stimulus with a 15-beats-per-minute increase. Ordinarily we might conclude that individual *B* is the more responsive. However, if the range of heart rates that *A* is capable of (his maximum minus his minimum) is 50 beats per minute, while *B*'s range is 100 beats per minute, we might conclude that *A* is more responsive. That is, *A*'s response of 10 beats per minute represents 10/50, 20 percent of his range, while *B*'s response of 15 beats per minute represents only 15/100, 15 percent of his range. A similar line of reasoning applies to resting levels of autonomic activity.

Lykken's suggestion that autonomic activity should be "corrected for individual differences in range was used in a study discussed on p. 41 (Hare, 1968a). Hare's data had been expressed in the usual way, that is uncorrected for range (see Table 3 and Figures 6 and 9). Some of these data, however, were also expressed as range-corrected scores. The maximum skin conductance and heart rate that occurred while each subject blew up a balloon to bursting were taken as crude estimates of the maximum activity in these two systems. Minimum activity was simply the lowest level of skin conductance and heart rate that occurred during the course of the experiment.

Each individual's resting skin conductance and heart rate were converted into range-corrected scores by the formula

$$\phi = \frac{\text{resting level} - \text{minimum level}}{\text{maximum level} - \text{minimum level}} \tag{1}$$

Where ϕ is the *resting level,* expressed as a proportion of the individual's range, and can vary in value from 0.0 to 1.0. Similarly, each individual's responses to several of the stimuli used in the experiment were converted to range-corrected change or response scores by the formula

$$\Delta\phi = \frac{\text{stimulus level} - \text{prestimulus level}}{\text{maximum level} - \text{minimum level}} \tag{2}$$

where $\Delta\phi$ is the *magnitude of change,* expressed as a proportion of an individual's range. To facilitate comparison, both uncorrected and corrected skin conductance and heart rate data are presented together in Table 4 (the uncorrected data are taken from Table 3). It is noteworthy that the psychopaths had the lowest resting skin conductance when uncorrected units were used, but that correction for range removed this difference. However, there was a tendency, in range-corrected responses to auditory stimuli, for the nonpsychopaths to be the most responsive, the psychopaths the least responsive, and the mixed group somewhere in between. This ap-

TABLE 4: Skin Conductance and Heart Rate Data Expressed in Absolute Units and as a Function of Individual Range (After Hare, 1968a.)

Variable	Group		
	Psychopaths	Mixed Group	Nonpsychopaths
Resting skin conductance			
Raw units	1.20	1.18	1.42
ϕ	0.08	0.09	0.06
Resting heart rate			
Raw units	78.8	73.6	75.4
ϕ	0.31	0.30	0.33
GSR to Tone 1			
Raw units	0.12	0.13	0.11
$\Delta\phi$	0.17	0.22	0.25
Cardiac response to Tone 1			
Raw units	4.2	4.7	6.3
$\Delta\phi$	0.08	0.07	0.15
GSR to Tone 16			
Raw units	0.07	0.07	0.08
$\Delta\phi$	0.09	0.13	0.16
Cardiac response to Tone 16			
Raw units	3.3	4.6	6.2
$\Delta\phi$	0.05	0.07	0.12

plied to both skin conductance (GSR) and heart rate changes, although the trend was more pronounced for the latter.

If Lykken's rationale is accepted, these results may be taken as support for the hypothesis that the primary psychopath is both sympathetically (GSR) and parasympathetically (cardiac deceleration) underreactive to simple auditory stimulation.

RECOVERY FROM STRESS

Besides the psychopath's resting autonomic state and his responsivity to stimulation, we can consider whether he differs from others in the rate at which he recovers from the effects of stimulation. In doing so, we make use of a theory of autonomic dysfunction developed by Rubin (1965). Although the theory is confined to psychoneurotic behavior, it has some interesting implications for psychopathy.

Rubin assumes that an important feature of neurotic behavior is slow homeostatic recovery (restoration of equilibrium between SNS and PNS activity) following aversive stimulation or stress. This assumption is based on his finding that during periods of relaxation and painful stimulation, the pattern of adrenergic (sympathetic) and cholinergic (parasympathetic) activity is the same for neurotic subjects as it is for normal ones. For both groups of subjects the typical response to painful stimulation or stress is an increase in adrenergic and a decrease in cholinergic activity. However, following the termination of the stimulation, the autonomic activity of the normal subjects quickly returns to prestimulus levels, while that of the neurotic subjects does not. That is, neurotics give the appropriate autonomic response to painful stimulation, but with the termination of this stimulation they continue to respond autonomically as if it were still present. One of the behavioral consequences of this failure of emotional activity to subside once the danger is past is the opportunity for many internal and external cues to become associated with internal emotional (autonomic) responses:

> . . . one would predict that persons possessing such an aberrant autonomic propensity would inevitably respond to many more aspects of their environment with heightened internal emotional responses (fear, apprehension, anxiety) than would normal individuals (1965, p. 225).

Experiments recently reviewed by Malmo (1966) are consistent with Rubin's hypothesis, and suggest further that the augmented muscle-tension that occurs during states of anxiety and in response to stressful stimulation may also be persistent in psychoneurotics. The relevance of Rubin's theory to psychopathy is that some of the characteristics of the psychopath are more or less opposite to those of the neurotic. We might therefore expect that, whereas the autonomic correlates of fear subside slowly in the neurotic, they subside very rapidly in the psychopath. That is, we might expect that even if the psychopath gives the appropriate autonomic responses to stressful stimuli, he recovers very quickly.

Although not very extensive, some pertinent experimental evidence does exist. As mentioned earlier, Lindner (1942) presented psychopathic and nonpsychopathic criminals with a series of tones and electric shocks. He found that after a shock the skin resistance of the psychopaths took *longer* to return to a prestimulus level than did that of the nonpsychopaths. That is, contrary to what we would expect, the psychopaths recovered slowly, more or less the way a neurotic (according to Rubin's theory) might behave. However, at the end of the experiment, presumably when they knew that tones and shocks were no longer being given, the psychopaths showed ". . . a decidedly increased facility to revert to a normal mode of physiological functioning at the *conclusion* of an emotionally charged episode (p. 275)." Thus the psychopaths recovered slowly after a noxious stimulus but rapidly to termination of a *stressful situation*. It is difficult to draw any real conclusions from Lindner's study, since his psychopathic group was poorly defined and probably included a number of neurotic criminals. However, in a more recent study Hare (1965c) failed to find any difference in the rate at which the skin conductance of psychopaths and nonpsychopaths recovered from the effects of a strong electric shock (see Chapter 4 for more detail). In a study by Lippert and Senter (1966) psychopathic and nonpsychopathic subjects were told that at the end of a 10-minute period (a clock was in view) they would receive a strong electric shock through electrodes attached to the leg (stress period). No shock was actually administered. The degree of spontaneous (nonspecific) GSR activity was taken as the indicant of sympathetic arousal. Spontaneous GSR activity increased in both groups during the stress period, with the psychopaths showing a smaller increase. During the 10 minutes following the stress period, the spontaneous GSR activity of both groups decreased. However, the activity of the nonpsychopaths still remained somewhat above what it had been during the prestress (resting) period, while that of the psychopaths *dropped well below* the prestress period. Lippert and Senter interpret these results to indicate that the psychopath ". . . shows less tendency to respond in anticipation of future shock or to continue to respond after stimulation has passed (1966, p. 26)."

Taken together, these studies provide no support for the hypothesis that the psychopath recovers quickly from the effects of a specific noxious stimulus. However, when a stressful situation is involved instead of a specific stimulus, there is some evidence that, with the termination of the situation, psychopaths exhibit the sort of rapid autonomic recovery that we might expect on the basis of Rubin's theory. Still, the paucity of relevant research makes any conclusions highly tentative. What is particularly needed are studies in which autonomic responses (for example, heart rate, pupil diameter) that depend on dual sympathetic and parasympathetic innervation are monitored.

PHARMACOLOGICAL STUDIES

Several investigators have used drugs as a basis for inferences about ANS activity in psychopaths.

One of the drugs that has been used is *mecholyl,* a substance that produces a drop in blood pressure (because it increases parasympathetic activity). There are individual differences in the magnitude and duration of blood pressure change following the injection of mecholyl. For our purposes, the two most important patterns are the *Type N* and the *Type E*. A Type N response consists of a small, temporary reduction in blood pressure; it reflects a compensatory increase in sympathetic activity and a rapid return to a balanced (homeostatic) autonomic state within the organism. A Type E response consists of a large, prolonged drop in blood pressure; it reflects a relatively slow return to a balanced autonomic state (King, 1958).

Besides being indicative of autonomic responsivity and homeostatic recovery, there is some evidence that blood pressure responses to mecholyl are predictive of how an individual will react to stress. During periods of stress, Type N responders tend to become aggressive, while Type E responders tend to become anxious (Fine and Sweeney, 1968).

Gellhorn (1957) administered mecholyl to 104 normal subjects and a group of psychiatric patients, including 37 criminals diagnosed as psychopathic (the criteria for diagnosis were not given). Type N responses were given by 46 percent of the psychopathic subjects and by 22 percent of the normal subjects, while Type E responses were given by 16 percent of the psychopaths and 7 percent of the normal subjects. The relatively large percentage of Type N responses given by the psychopathic group is consistent with the research in which psychopaths showed rapid homeostatic recovery following termination of a stressful situation, and is also consistent with clinical observations that psychopaths are frequently aggressive. The fact that 16 percent of Gellhorn's psychopathic group gave Type E responses, indicative of slow homeostatic recovery and a tendency toward anxiety during stress, suggests that these subjects may actually have been neurotic criminals instead of psychopathic ones.

Kaplan (1960) also administered mecholyl to a group of criminals. Subjects who gave a Type N response (psychopaths?) tended to be aggressive, while those who gave a Type E response (neurotic criminals?) tended to be more anxious. The use of a depressant (either sodium amytal or chlorpromazine) served to increase the magnitude of Type N response and to make the subjects even more aggressive. Assuming that the Type N responders were mainly psychopaths, the effects of a depressant are consistent with the frequent observation (see, for example, Cleckley, 1964) that alcohol quickly causes psychopaths to lose whatever behavioral inhibitions they may have had. Kaplan also found that depressants changed some Type E responses to Type N responses; associated with this change was a tendency for the subjects to become less anxious and more aggressive. The results of a study by Blackburn (1968) indicated that the aggressive behavior of some criminals reflected a breakdown of strong inhibitions after prolonged or repeated provocation. These individuals tended to be neurotic rather than psychopathic. It is possible, therefore, that the Type E responders in Kaplan's study become more aggressive under the influence of depressants because these drugs served to reduce their inhibitions and control over aggressive behavior.

Before concluding this section, it is worth noting that aggressiveness and anxiety are related not only to the type of blood pressure response to mecholyl, but also to the relative concentrations of the catecholamines, adrenalin, and noradrenalin, within the body (Fine and Sweeney, 1968; Schildkraut and Kety, 1967). In general, aggressiveness, either as a momentary state or as a personality trait, appears to be related to large concentrations of noradrenalin, while anxiety is related to large concentrations of adrenalin. We might therefore expect to find that psychopaths, particularly the more aggressive ones, give Type N responses to mecholyl and are characterized by a relatively high concentration of noradrenalin within the body. Neurotic delinquents, on the other hand, should give Type E responses to mecholyl and be characterized by a high concentration of adrenalin within the body.

SUMMARY

Although the number of relevant studies is not very large, several tentative conclusions about the relationship between psychopathy and autonomic functioning are possible.

During periods of relative quiescence psychopathic subjects tend to be hypoactive on several indices of autonomic activity, including resting level of skin conductance and autonomic variability ("spontaneous" fluctuations in electrodermal and cardiac activity). Although these findings must be interpreted with caution, they are at least consistent with most clinical statements about the psychopath's general lack of anxiety, guilt, and emotional "tension."

The situation with respect to autonomic responsivity is more complex. Nevertheless, it appears that psychopaths may give relatively small electrodermal responses to "lie detection" situations and to situations that would ordinarily be considered stressful. They may also exhibit rapid electrodermal recovery at the termination of stressful situations.

Finally, there is some evidence (although scant) that psychopaths give a blood pressure response to injection of mecholyl that is indicative of rapid homeostatic recovery and a tendency to become aggressive under stress.

CHAPTER FIVE

PSYCHOPATHY AND THE CONCEPT OF AROUSAL

So far we have considered some of the empirical evidence for the existence of cortical and autonomic correlates of psychopathy. Much of this evidence is relevant to the hypothesis held by several investigators that certain aspects of the psychopath's behavior are related to a relatively low level of·*cortical arousal* or *activation.*

THE CONCEPT OF AROUSAL

Many investigators have suggested that stimulation has two main effects on an individual. First, stimuli function as cues for the guidance and regulation of behavior, an effect that is largely dependent on learning and experience. The second effect of stimulation is to increase the individual's level of activation or arousal.

Arousal can be defined as a dimension representing the physiological and psychological state of an organism. The low end of the dimension is characterized by deep sleep, complete loss of awareness, and a low level of physiological activity [1] (see Table 5). As arousal increases, the individual's awareness of the environment and his behavioral efficiency also increases,

---

[1] As measured by EEG patterns (see Figure 4), muscle tension, and autonomic activity (such as skin conductance, heart rate). But see p. 68.

TABLE 5: Levels of Arousal and Their EEG, Psychological, and Behavioral Correlates (Modified from Lindsley, 1952.)

Level of Arousal	Behavioral Continuum	EEG	State of Awareness	Behavioral Efficiency
High	Strong, excited emotion (fear, rage, anxiety)	Desynchronized: Low to moderate amplitude; fast, mixed frequencies.	Restricted awareness: Divided attention; diffuse, hazy; "confusion."	Poor (lack of control, freezing-up, disorganized).
	Alert attentiveness	Partially synchronized: Mainly fast, low amplitude waves.	Selective attention, but may vary or shift. "Concentration" anticipation, "set."	Good (efficient, selective, quick, reactions).
	Relaxed wakefulness	Synchronized: Optimal alpha rhythm.	Attention wanders—not forced. Favors free association.	Good (routine reactions and creative thought).
	Drowsiness	Reduced alpha and occasional low aplitude slow waves.	Borderline, partial awareness. Imagery and reverie. "Dreamlike states."	Poor (uncoordinated, sporadic, lacking sequential timing).
	Light sleep	Spindle bursts and slow waves (larger), loss of alphas.	Markedly reduced consciousness (loss of consciousness). Dream state.	Absent
Low	Deep sleep	Large and very slow waves.	Complete loss of awareness (no memory for stimulation or for dreams).	Absent

but only up to a point—at very high levels of arousal awareness and efficiency tend to break down. This relationship between arousal and behavioral efficiency, often described as an "inverted **u** function," is plotted in

Figure 10. It is evident that states of arousal above and below some optimal level are related to progressive decreases in the efficiency of behavior. A similar relationship exists between level of arousal and affective experience—both high and low levels of arousal are much more unpleasant than some more moderate level (see the right side of Figure 10). One implication of this latter relationship is that an individual in too low a state of arousal will probably seek to *increase* arousal; one who is in too heightened a state of arousal will probably seek to *decrease* it. That is, organisms tend to seek and maintain some optimal level of arousal. A related implication is that changes in arousal *toward* the optimal level ought to be *rewarding,* while changes *away* from the optimal level ought to be *punishing.* Since one of the major determinants of arousal is stimulation, we would expect an individual either to seek stimulation or to avoid it, depending on whether he is below or above what is for him (at any given time) an optimal level of arousal.

Before relating the foregoing discussion to psychopathy, a few comments are needed about the way in which stimulation influences arousal. As Figure 11 illustrates, the neural pathways running from a sensory receptor (A) to the appropriate part of the cortex (B) send off branches into the *reticular formation,* an important mechanism within the brain stem. When a sensory receptor is stimulated, therefore, information about the stimulus is carried to the cortex, and at the same time the reticular formation is stimulated into activity. The reticular formation in turns sends excitatory signals to all areas of the cortex; the result is a general increase in cortical arousal. At the same time, the reticular formation can induce ac-

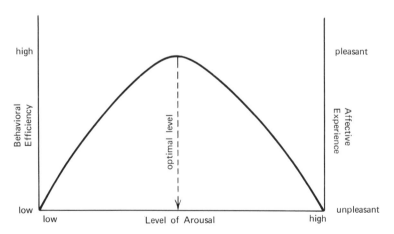

FIGURE 10. Hypothetical curve relating level of arousal to behavioral efficiency and affective experience.

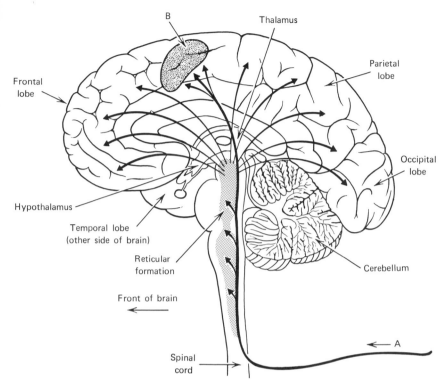

FIGURE 11. **Diagram showing the relationship between sensory pathways (A to B) and the reticular formation.**

tivity in other parts of the brain concerned with increasing autonomic and muscular activity and decreasing sensory thresholds. The individual becomes more alert and sensitive to stimulation, especially the stimulation that had initially activated the reticular formation (recall the concept of the OR, discussed on p. 47).

The reticular formation can also *decrease* cortical, autonomic, and behavioral arousal and raise sensory thresholds. Similarly, it is able to monitor incoming signals, allowing those that are significant and relevant to the organism to pass and filtering out those that are not significant or relevant. The habituation of the OR (see p. 47), for example, probably reflects the tendency of the reticular formation to filter out stimuli that are repetitive and have therefore lost their novelty and significance to the individual. This means that the reticular formation is most likely to increase arousal not only when stimulation is relatively intense, but also when it is meaningful, complex, surprising, incongruous, novel, variable, puzzling, and so on. That these properties of stimulation do in fact increase arousal has been demonstrated in a variety of contexts (Berlyne, 1966; Fiske and Maddi, 1961).

Although the discussion so far has emphasized the reticular formation's role in regulating cortical, autonomic, muscular, and sensory functions, we should point out that these same functions can in turn influence reticular activity. Cortical activity (thoughts, ideas), for example, can stimulate the reticular formation, which in turn can either facilitate or inhibit further cortical, autonomic, and muscular activity. Similarly, increases in autonomic activity can result in an increase in reticular and cortical activity, a point to which we shall shortly return.

PSYCHOPATHY, AROUSAL, AND NEED FOR STIMULATION

Several investigators have hypothesized that psychopathy is related to a lowered state of cortical arousal and to a chronic need for stimulation. Quay (1965), for example, suggested that it is possible to view the psychopath's impulsivity, need for excitement, and inability to tolerate routine and boredom as the result of a pathological need for stimulation. Compared to ordinary individuals, the psychopath needs a greater level and variety of sensory input to maintain positive affect or an optimal level of arousal. As we have just seen, intense and varied stimulation can in fact increase reticular activity and cortical arousal.

Petrie (1967) also described the psychopath in terms of a need for stimulation. She assumed that individuals differ in the degree and direction of sensory modulation—*reducers* subjectively reduce the intensity of environmental stimulation while *augmenters* subjectively increase it. According to Petrie, the psychopath is a reducer and consequently in a state of actual or threatened stimulus deprivation.

Petrie's reducer-augmenter distinction is similar to Lykken's (1968) concept of *preception*. Preception is described as a kind of "afferent tuning" that attenuates (negative preception) or enhances (positive preception) sensory input in proportion to the individual's ability to predict the source, quality, and time of occurrence of a stimulus. For example, a brief warning signal prior to an electric shock has been found to reduce the magnitude of GSR to shock. Generally, we would expect that intense or noxious stimulation would be preceded by negative preception, but that some individuals would be more efficient at preception than would others. Lykken [2] has suggested, for example, that psychopaths may be particularly efficient

[2] Personal communication, 1967.

at negative preception, with the result that the subjective intensity (and perhaps the psychological significance) of painful stimulation is lessened.

Lykken's concept of negative preception is similar to classical conditioning paradigms in which a warning signal (CS) is followed by a noxious stimulus (UCS). Recall that in such a paradigm the CS may acquire inhibitory properties that reduce the unconditioned response (UCR) to the UCS (see p. 51). If the psychopath is indeed efficient at negative preception (or at acquiring strong CS-related inhibitory potentials), we would expect him to give small UCRs to noxious stimuli that are preceded by an appropriate warning signal. As we saw earlier (p. 51), this is what Lykken (1955) did, in fact, find in a classical GSR conditioning experiment using shock as the UCS. However, we have no way of knowing whether this means that the psychopaths were particularly adept at negative preception or whether they were simply less reactive to shock than were the nonpsychopaths, since preception and reactivity in this experiment were confounded.

In many respects Eysenck's (1967) theory of personality bears on arousal theories of psychopathy. For example, one of the main personality dimensions in Eysenck's theory is *extraversion,* a dimension that he has recently related to reticular-cortical arousal—extraverts fall at the low end and introverts at the high end of the arousal continuum. In terms of cortical arousal then, extraverts and psychopaths appear to be similar. Eysenck refers to the psychopath as a *neurotic extravert.* The difficulty here lies in the use of his term neurotic. In Eysenck's theory, *neuroticism* or emotionality is related to lability and instability of the autonomic nervous system. As we have seen (Chapter 4), there is little evidence to support his contention that psychopaths are autonomically labile; on the contrary, it appears that they are autonomically underreactive. This discrepancy may reflect the possibility that what Eysenck refers to as psychopaths are, in fact, neurotic delinquents (see p. 7). Within the context of his theory, therefore, it may be more appropriate to refer to psychopaths as *stable extraverts.* At the same time, we should not push the analogy between extraversion and psychopathy too far. Although both are presumably related to cortical underarousal, psychopathy involves a great deal more than this.[3]

Level of Cortical Arousal

Earlier (p. 62) we noted that activation of the autonomic nervous system can increase reticular and cortical arousal. To elaborate somewhat, there is some evidence (see Lacey and Lacey, 1958) that fluctuations in skin conductance and heart rate (that is, autonomic variability) have excita-

[3] Schoenherr (1964) found that the mean extraversion and neuroticism scores of psychopathic and nonpsychopathic criminals were no higher than those obtained by the normal population. That is, psychopaths were neither neurotic nor extraverted.

tory effects on the cortex. Since psychopaths appear to be characterized by relatively little autonomic variability (see p. 43), this source of cortical arousal would be less effective for them than it would be for normal subjects.

It is worth recalling here that the pattern of autonomic responsivity observed in psychopaths during repetitive stimulation was similar to that observed in subjects who gave EEG indications of drowsiness (see p. 48).

Besides this presumptive evidence of cortical underarousal based on the relationship between autonomic and cortical activity, several EEG and perceptual studies are of interest. For example, the evidence that psychopaths exhibit excessive amounts of slow-wave activity (see p. 30) and that they give smaller than normal cortical evoked potentials to the second of two stimuli (see p. 34) is consistent with the hypothesis that they are in a state of low cortical arousal. Some related evidence comes from a study in which the *two-flash threshold* (TFT) was used as an indicant of cortical arousal (Rose, 1964). The TFT is the minimum interval of time required for two brief flashes of light to be seen as a double instead of a single flash. When the interval between successive flashes is very small, an alert, aroused subject is more likely to perceive two flashes than is a less aroused subject; that is, the higher the level of arousal, the lower the TFT is likely to be. Rose found that psychiatric patients with a low TFT tended to be anxious, agitated, and depressed, while those with a high TFT tended to be less anxious, more impulsive, and psychopathic. Thus, psychopathy was related to low cortical arousal as determined by the TFT.

Sensitivity to Stimulation

There is some experimental evidence that arousal is negatively correlated not only with the TFT but also with stimulus-*detection* thresholds. Edelberg (1961) found that increases in skin conductance and decreases in the volume of the blood vessels in the fingers were associated with a drop in tactile threshold, a relationship that was, in part, interpreted as reflecting ". . . cortical arousal associated concurrently with autonomic activity and increased perceptivity" (p. 193). Similarly, Silverman, Cohen, and Shmavonian (1959) found that increased GSR activity was related to a decrease in the threshold for detection of electric shock. In the light of these findings, we would expect the psychopath's low level of arousal to be associated with relatively high stimulus-detection thresholds. The results of several studies are consistent with this expectation (Hare, 1968b; Schoenherr, 1964). In each case, psychopaths had a higher shock-detection threshold than did nonpsychopaths.

What about *tolerance* for strong or painful stimulation? If psychopaths are indeed less receptive to stimulation, we would expect that any given intensity of stimulation would be subjectively less intense to a psychopath than to others. Results consistent with this expectation were obtained by Schalling and Levander (1964); predominantly nonanxious, psychopathic delinquents had higher pain and tolerance thresholds for electric shock than did anxious, nonpsychopathic delinquents. Several other studies, however, have found no appreciable differences between psychopaths and nonpsychopaths either in their tolerance for shock (Hare, 1965c, 1966a; Schoenherr, 1964) or in their "painfulness" ratings of a shock of given intensity (Schachter and Latane, 1964). One of the difficulties here is that, as most clinicians will acknowledge, the psychopath is unlikely to accept any more pain than he has to. Thus it is possible that in the latter four studies the psychopaths *could* have tolerated more shock than the nonpsychopaths, but that they preferred not to. Clearly, more research is needed in which motivational variables are manipulated.[4]

Need for Stimulation

We have seen that a number of investigators consider the psychopath to be an individual who cannot tolerate routine and boredom and who continually seems in need of "extra" stimulation. Many clinicians would agree, although not necessarily for the reasons discussed earlier (arousal, cortical inhibition, preception, reducer, and so forth). Cleckley (1964), for example, says of the psychopath,

> Being bored, he will seek to cut up more than the ordinary person in order to relieve the tedium of his unrewarding existence [p. 426]. . . . Perhaps the emptiness or superficiality of a life without major goals or deep loyalties, or real love, would leave a person with high intelligence and other superior qualities so bored that he would eventually turn to hazardous, self-damaging, outlandish, antisocial, and even destructive exploits in order to find something fresh and stimulating in which to apply his useless and unchallenged energies and talents (p. 441).

Assuming that the psychopath is in fact easily bored, he should perform poorly on tasks that are inherently tedious and monotonous. Tasks of this sort are commonly used in experimental studies of *vigilance* in which the subject is required to detect transient signals appearing against a relatively unchanging background, such as monitoring a radar screen for long periods of time. There is some evidence that the performance decrement that usually occurs during these vigilance tasks is associated with a corresponding decrease in cortical and autonomic arousal. Therefore, we might expect that psychopaths, with their low level of cortical and autonomic

[4]A recent study by Hare and Thorvaldson (in press) found that concrete incentives induced psychopaths to accept significantly stronger shocks than those accepted by nonpsychopaths.

arousal, would do poorly on monotonous vigilance tasks. The results of a recent study are consistent with this expectation. Orris (1967) found that psychopathic delinquents performed less well (detected fewer signals) in a simple visual monitoring task than did other delinquents. Presumably the lack of varied stimulus input in this monotonous task served to keep the psychopaths' level of arousal below that needed for efficient performance (see Figure 7). A related possibility, suggested by Orris, is that the psychopaths' proneness to boredom led them to engage in self-stimulating activity (singing, talking, looking around) that interfered with the vigilance task.

Several investigators have attempted to determine whether the psychopath does in fact actually *seek* stimulation. On the basis of Petrie's conception of the psychopath as a reducer of stimulation and the neurotic as an augmenter, Wiesen (1965) hypothesized that a simple lever-pressing response would be learned by psychopaths when *onset* of stimulation was the reinforcer, while neurotics would learn the response with cessation of stimulation as the reinforcer. Stimulation in this case was either mechanical (colored lights and a radio) or human (the experimenter waving and nodding at the subject). The subjects, university students selected on the basis of MMPI criteria of psychopathy and neuroticism, performed as predicted when stimulation was mechanical but not when it was human.

We mentioned earlier (p. 61) that level of arousal is related not only to the intensity of stimulation, but also to its novelty, complexity, meaningfulness, and so on. It follows that a subject wishing to decrease arousal should prefer familiar, simple stimulation. To put it another way, there should be a negative correlation between level of arousal and the degree of novelty and complexity preferred. Empirical support for this postulated relationship has been provided by the results of several studies (see Berlyne, 1966).

If the psychopath is characterized by a low arousal level he should show more of a preference for novel and complex stimulation than should neurotic persons. A study by Skrzypek (1969) tested this prediction. The subjects were psychopathic and neurotic delinquents selected on the basis of scores on Quay's (1964) behavior-rating checklist. Preference for novelty was determined by presenting each subject with 12 pairs of pictures (one member of each pair being novel and the other familiar) and counting the number of times that he chose the novel picture. Similarly, preference for complexity was determined by counting the number of times that the more complex member of 28 pairs of random shapes was chosen. In addition, a self-report measure of anxiety was administered. After completing the novelty, complexity, and anxiety pretests, the subjects were randomly assigned to one of three conditions: (1) *perceptual isolation* (40 minutes in the dark), (2) *arousal* (a series of progressively more difficult auditory discriminations with reward for correct responses and punishment for incorrect responses); (3) *control* (40 minutes on a pursuit-rotor task). Following this, posttest measures of anxiety and preference for novelty and complexity were taken.

The results were as follows: (1) For all 66 subjects, anxiety was significantly and negatively correlated with preference for complexity, thus supporting studies in which level of arousal and preference for complexity and novelty were negatively correlated; (2) the psychopathic delinquents were considerably less anxious than were the neurotic delinquents; (3) during the pretest, the psychopaths showed greater preference for complexity and novelty than did the neurotics; (4) perceptual isolation produced greater increases in preference for complexity in the psychopaths than in the neurotics; (5) arousal had no effect on the psychopaths but it produced a significant increase in the anxiety of the neurotics and a decrease in their preference for complexity. In general then, the results support the hypothesis that, compared to the neurotic delinquent, the psychopathic delinquent is in a state of cortical underarousal and sensory deprivation.

Presumably, much of the psychopath's behavior serves to increase sensory input and arousal to more optimal levels. Situations that most people find frightening may simply be "exciting" to a psychopath and consequently actively sought out by him. Therefore, we would expect that given the choice between an activity that is normally thought of as frightening and one that is safe but dull, the psychopath, more than the nonpsychopath, would prefer the former. Besides the clinical impressions in support of this expectation, some relevant empirical data are available. Lykken (1955) constructed an activity preference questionnaire that consisted of 33 forced-choice items. Samples of these items are as follows:

3. (a) Having to cancel your vacation ;
   (b) Standing on the ledge of the 25th floor of a building.
7. (a) Spending an evening with some boring people;
   (b) Being seen naked by a neighbor.

Each item thus consisted of a frightening and nonfrightening activity, previously matched for unpleasantness. As we might expect, psychopaths showed a significantly greater preference for the frightening items than did either neurotic criminals or normal noncriminals.

There are other ways in which psychopaths could increase cortical arousal. One way would be to resort to self-generated stimulation, especially when appropriate sources of external stimulation are not available. This would perhaps explain the tendency of the psychopathic subjects in Orris' (1967) study to engage in self-stimulating activities (singing, talking) during a boring vigilance task (see p. 66). Another source of internal stimulation might be fantasy and daydreaming. In this case we would expect the psychopath's fantasy to be concerned with highly exciting and stimulating topics instead of with "vicarious trial and error" in which various courses of action and their possible consequences are run through mentally beforehand (see p. 23).

Another way of increasing sensory input and cortical arousal would be through the use of psychoactive stimulant drugs, such as amphetamines. These drugs appear to selectively increase cortical and behavioral arousal and responsivity to environmental stimuli (Irwin, 1968), and for these reasons should be very appealing to psychopaths.[5] Psychopaths should also be attracted to psychotomimetic drugs, such as mescaline, LSD-25, and psilocybin, which greatly increase cortical arousal. The intense and varied auditory, visual, and self-generated stimulation associated with psychedelic music and dancing should also be very appealing to them. On the other hand, we might expect psychopaths to avoid barbiturate-type drugs, tranquilizers (such as chlorpromazine), and narcotics (for example, opium, morphine, methadone), since these drugs all reduce arousal. The results of several studies are consistent with these suggestions. Hill (1947), for example, found that amphetamine produced at least a temporary improvement in the behavior of aggressive psychopaths.[6] On the other hand, Cleckley (1964), among others, commented that even small amounts of alcohol (a cortical depressant) appear to facilitate the antisocial behavior of psychopaths. More recently, Robins (1966) found that only a very small percentage of psychopaths used opiates, barbiturates, bromides, or tranquilizers.

A somewhat related source of stimulation would be that associated with *dreaming*. There is abundant evidence that the rapid-eye-movement (REM) period of the sleep cycle (during which highly organized, imagery-laden dream activity occurs) is characterized by intense midbrain, reticular, and cortical activity (see Ephron and Carrington, 1966). It appears that the excitation provided by REM sleep serves to maintain the central nervous system at an optimal level of functioning during the waking state. After discussing, among other things, evidence that the proportion of the sleep cycle that is given to REM sleep is very great at birth and decreases with age, Roffwarg, Muzio, and Dement (1966) suggested that the activity

[5] It has been suggested that the paradoxical sedative effect that the amphetamines have on the hyperactive, brain-damaged child may be related to the ability of these drugs to increase cortical and behavioral arousal, thereby bringing the child up to his optimal level of arousal (Irwin, 1968).

[6] It is of interest here that amphetamine can produce a shift in EEG activity from slow waves to fast waves (Barnes, 1966).

associated with REM sleep may also play an important role in neural development.

> We have hypothesized that the REM mechanism serves as an endogenous source of functional excitation, furnishing great quantities of functional excitation to higher centers. Such stimulation would be particularly crucial during the periods *in utero* and shortly after birth, before appreciable exogenous stimulation is available to the central nervous system. It might assist in the structural maturation and differentiation of key sensory and motor areas within the central nervous system . . . (p. 617).

How is all this relevant to psychopathy? One possibility is that the psychopath's lowered cortical arousal and need for sensory input are related to disturbances in REM sleep activity. If, for some reason, he does not get enough REM sleep, he may have to make up for it by obtaining inordinate amounts of sensory input during the waking hours. One way of doing so might be to engage in activities that are considered dangerous, foolish, or impulsive by others, but that are exciting to the psychopath.

Modulation of Sensory Input

Much of the discussion so far indicates that psychopathy may be related to a general tendency to attenuate sensory input. There would be several interesting consequences of this tendency. First, many of the cues essential for adequate social functioning are subtle and of low intensity. The psychopath's tendency to attenuate sensory input would mean that some of these cues would be below threshold and relatively ineffective. Further, in an attempt to attain an optimal level of arousal, the psychopath is likely to actively seek intense stimulation or at least stimulation that has "exciting" or arousing qualities. In scanning the environment for such stimulation, however, he would probably miss, or perhaps simply ignore, many social cues—cues that have important informational and emotional content and are needed for the guidance of behavior. As a result, he would ordinarily be little influenced by many of the cues emanating from other individuals. If, however, these cues had special significance for him—as would be the case if he were trying to use others for his own purposes—we might expect that a special effort would be made to attend to them.

Besides a general tendency to attenuate sensory input, it is possible that psychopaths are able to *selectively* modulate input; in effect, they may be able to "tune out" or at least greatly attenuate stimulation that is potentially disturbing (see p. 35). The result would be that threats of punishment and cues warning of unpleasant consequences for misbehavior would not have the same emotional impact that they would have for other individuals. Paradoxically, this would mean that cues that are a source of emotional (and cortical) arousal for normal persons would not have the same function with psychopaths, the very ones who are most in need of this arousal.

DETERMINANTS OF DIFFERENCES
IN PHYSIOLOGICAL FUNCTIONING

We have seen that a considerable amount of evidence leads to a conclusion that there are cortical and autonomic differences between psychopathic and normal individuals. The problem now becomes one of explaining how these differences arise. A related problem, not confined to psychopathy, concerns the extent to which personality traits and mental disorders are influenced by hereditary mechanisms (see Eysenck, 1967; Vandenberg, 1966).

Although EEG activity is complex and not well understood, there is some evidence indicating that its determinants are partly hereditary in nature. With respect to psychopathy, the similarity between the EEGs of parents and their offspring has been the subject of a considerable amount of research. Typical of this research is a study by Knott et al. (1953) in which the EEG records of 86 psychopaths and their true parents were compared. The distributions of EEG types obtained from these two groups of subjects, along with a corresponding distribution obtained from a large normal population, clearly indicated that there was an excess of EEG abnormality in both the psychopathic group and in the true parents of this group, although the deviations from normality were somewhat greater in the former. In each case, the dominant type of abnormality was the presence of slow-wave activity. Moreover, there was a significant tendency for the psychopathic patients with slow waves to have parents with slow waves, and for patients with fast waves to have parents with fast waves. Since Knott et al. found no relationship between the EEG records of psychopathic patients (N = 9) and those of their foster parents (N = 18), they concluded that their results supported the hypothesis that there are genetic determinants of EEG activity. To the extent that slow-wave activity is related to cortical immaturity and/or underarousal, and assuming that these are related to some aspects of psychopathic behavior, we might conclude that the development of psychopathy is influenced by genetic determinants. It is relevant here that besides slow-wave activity, several other variables usually associated with arousal (for example, some sensory thresholds) appear to have hereditary components (see Vandenberg, 1966), again suggesting that at least part of the cortical differences between psychopathic and other individuals is genetic in nature.

Alternative hypotheses are, of course, possible. For example, the concordance between the EEG patterns of parent and offspring found by Knott et al. (and by various other investigators) might arise from the effects of similar psychological environments instead of from the influences of genetic mechanisms. Similarly, the EEG abnormalities observed might simply represent the neurophysiological expression of psychological disturbances found in the parents and, through learning, in their children as well. Knott et al. considered hypotheses of this sort and rejected them, largely on the basis of their findings that the EEG patterns of patient and foster parents were dissimilar. However, the number of subjects involved was small, and no mention was made of the age at which the children had been placed with their foster parents. It is quite possible that any influence parents have on the EEG activity of their children is confined to the very early years. Recent research reported by Miller (1966) indicates that mechanisms by which parents influence their offsprings' EEG activity may in fact exist. In this research the brain-wave activity of rats was monitored, and whenever slow-wave activity was observed it was reinforced by direct electrical stimulation of rewarding areas in the brain. Other rats were reinforced for fast-wave activity. In each case the results indicated that the use of this instrumental learning technique could modify brain-wave activity; that is, either slow- or fast-wave activity could be learned. On the basis of these results, Miller suggested that it was possible that in the course of being rewarded for certain overt activities some people may learn a high level of arousal (that is, fast, low-voltage activity), while others may learn a low level of arousal (that is, slow, high-voltage activity). In regard to psychopathy, it is conceivable that the parents of psychopaths have consistently rewarded behavior that is associated with a low level of cortical arousal and that this is reflected in the slow-wave activity and cortical underarousal observed in psychopaths. Thus, although there is evidence that at least some of the cortical activity of psychopaths is the result of hereditary factors, it is probable that experiential and learning factors also play an important role.

Much the same situation exists with respect to autonomic functioning in the psychopath. Although no studies have involved psychopaths as subjects, several studies with normal subjects clearly point to the importance of hereditary mechanisms in determining the mode and patterning of autonomic activity (see, for example, Block, 1967; Vandenberg, 1966). Again, however, the influence of experiential factors must be considered, since evidence is rapidly accumulating to the effect that autonomic activity, similar to EEG patterns, can be manipulated by rewards and punishments (see review by Kimmel, 1967).

Before concluding this section, another fact requires brief mention.

Recent findings show that the presence of an extra Y chromosome in males (for example, XYY instead of the normal XY) may be related to extremely aggressive behavior (see the very readable account by Montagu, 1968). Whereas XYY chromosome complements are very rare in the normal population, it appears that this chromosome abnormality is found in about 2 to 3 percent of males whose behavior is so violent and aggressively antisocial that incarceration or institutionalization is required. In most cases these XYY males are over six feet tall, and they are frequently of subnormal intelligence. Whether the XYY complement is related to extremely aggressive forms of psychopathy (as opposed to other forms of criminal, antisocial behavior) is as yet unknown. Even if it is, the relationship would not really provide evidence one way or the other on the role of hereditary factors in psychopathy, since the XYY complement is not inherited—it apparently reflects the failure of the sex chromosomes to separate properly during formation of the sperm. Finally, the rarity of the disorder means that it could account for only a very small proportion of criminal behavior in general and aggressive psychopathy in particular.

SUMMARY

Several lines of research and theory suggest that psychopathy is related to cortical underarousal. As a result, the psychopath actively seeks stimulation with arousing or "exciting" qualities. In the process, however, he may be unaware of, or inattentive to, many of the subtle cues required for the guidance of behavior and for adequate social functioning.

CHAPTER SIX

PSYCHOPATHY AND LEARNING

Most attempts to account for psychopathic behavior in terms of learning theory have been based on one or the other of two general assumptions: that psychopathy is the product of a particular combination of early learning experiences; or that psychopathy is the result of an *inability* to learn certain forms of behavior necessary for efficient social functioning.

Social learning and environmental conceptions of psychopathy, based on the first assumption, are discussed in Chapter 7. The present chapter deals with attempts to test the hypothesis that the psychopath is characterized by some type of learning deficit.

Perhaps the most explicit statement of the learning deficit hypothesis has been made by Eysenck (1964). According to his view, the psychopath is an extravert (see p. 63) and therefore has a nervous system predisposed to the rapid development of cortical inhibitory potentials; as a result he acquires conditioned responses slowly and extinguishes them rapidly. Assuming that the process of socialization is dependent on conditioning, Eysenck concludes that the psychopath's undersocialization is the result of his inferior capacity for conditioning. Other investigators have tended to hold the question of predisposition in abeyance, and have looked for the particular conditions under which the psychopath may learn poorly. Several investigators have suggested that the main difference between psychopaths and others is in the difficulty with which the former acquire (1) classically conditioned fear responses; and (2) responses that appear to be mediated by fear or anxiety.

CLASSICAL CONDITIONING

Classical conditioning is a form of learning in which one stimulus acquires the capacity to elicit part of the response normally elicited by some other stimulus. For example, when the sound of a bell is repeatedly followed closely in time by the presentation of meat to a dog, part of the response generally elicited by the meat (for example, salivation) will eventually be elicited by the sound of the bell. In this case, the meat is called the unconditioned stimulus (UCS) and the response it elicits the unconditioned response (UCR). The bell, which normally does not produce salivation, is called the conditioned stimulus (CS), and the salivation that it elicits after repeated pairings with the UCS is referred to as the conditioned response (CR). In this example the CS apparently serves as a signal that the UCS is about to be presented, while the CR functions as a preparatory response in anticipation of the UCS. When a noxious or painful UCS (such as loud noise, electric shock, hard slap) is used, the CS may also appear to act as a partial substitute for the UCS. That is, the fear, anxiety, or distress elicited by the noxious UCS are also elicited, to a certain extent, by the CS. As we shall see, these conditioned emotional responses play an important role in the motivation and regulation of behavior.

The conditioning studies of psychopathy have generally used a noxious stimulus as the UCS (airpuff or electric shock) and either a skeletal-muscular response (eyeblink) or an autonomic response (GSR) as the response to be conditioned.

Eyeblink Conditioning

Miller (1966) used the MMPI (see p. 15) to select psychopathic and neurotic criminals; a third group of subjects consisted of ward attendants. In the conditioning procedure used, a light (CS) was followed 500 milliseconds later by an airpuff (UCS) directed at the cornea; the UCR to the airpuff was a reflexive eyeblink. A CR was defined as any eyeblink that occurred between 200 and 500 milliseconds after the onset of the light, a definition designed to eliminate the short-latency reflexive blinks that often occur to light in eyeblink experiments.

The results indicated that the psychopathic group contained more subjects who failed to condition (36 percent) than did either the neurotic group (15 percent) or the noncriminal group (23 percent); however, these differences between groups were not statistically significant.

Warren and Grant (1955) selected college students with high and low scores on the Psychopathic Deviate (Pd) scale of the MMPI. Unlike Miller's study, the Warren and Grant experiment included one session of *differential* conditioning. In this design one stimulus (the CS +) is followed by the UCS, whereas a noticeably different stimulus (the CS −) is not. In effect, the subject learns to respond with a CR to the CS + but not to the CS −. In the Warren and Grant study the conditioned stimuli were lights to the right and left of the subject's median plane of vision; the UCS was an airpuff. During the first day of conditioning, all *S*s were given 60 reinforced trials; that is, only the CS + and the UCS were presented. On the second day, 30 reinforced trials were interspersed with random presentations of the CS −. A CR was defined as any eyelid response with a latency of from 250 to 500 milliseconds after CS onset. The results, shown in Figure 12, indicated that there were no differences between groups during conditioning with only the CS + (Day 1), but that when differential conditioning was introduced (Day 2), an interesting difference emerged. The low-*Pd* subjects learned to discriminate between the CS + and the CS −; that is, they continued to respond to the CS + but showed a gradual decrease in responses to the CS −. The high-*Pd* subjects, on the other hand, did not show this differential responding. Warren and Grant interpreted these findings as providing support for the hypothesis that psychopaths, having learned an avoidance response to a noxious stimulus, fail to develop conditioned discrimination because of their tendency to avoid the discomfort associated with an airpuff by blinking indiscriminately to both

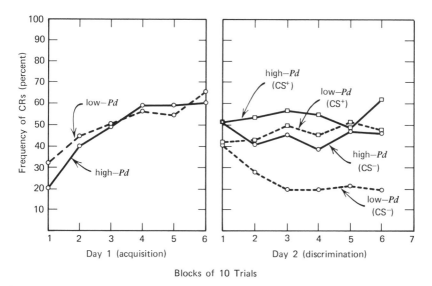

FIGURE 12. Acquisition of an eyelid CR (Day 1) and conditioned discrimination (Day 2) in high-*Pd* and low-*Pd* groups (after Warren and Grant, 1955).

the CS+ and the CS−. The implication here seems to be that the responses of some of the high-*Pd* subjects were partially voluntary in nature.

GSR Conditioning

Lykken's (1955) study is frequently cited in support of the contention that psychopaths acquire conditioned emotional (fear) responses slowly. The subjects in this study were psychopathic and neurotic criminals and normal noncriminals. The conditioning paradigm was somewhat similar to the eyeblink study by Warren and Grant (1955); both studies consisted of simple conditioning followed by differential conditioning.

The simple conditioning portion of Lykken's study consisted of seven presentations of a buzzer (CS+), each five seconds in duration, with an electric shock (UCS) administered just before the termination of each CS+. After this, in differential conditioning, four presentations of the CS+ and shock were interspersed with four unreinforced presentations of a different buzzer (CS−). A CR was defined as a GSR that occurred between the onset of the CS+ and the onset of the UCS, and was expressed as a proportion of the mean GSR elicited by the first six shocks. In extinction both stimuli were presented without shock, the CS+ 16 times and the CS− eight times.

Although the procedure and results were somewhat complex, several measures of conditioning clearly indicated that the psychopaths conditioned more slowly and extinguished [1] more rapidly than did either of the other two groups. On the assumption that GSR activity is a reasonable indicant of anxiety, Lykken interpreted these results as support for the hypothesis that psychopaths are defective in the acquisition of conditioned anxiety.

A study by Hare (1965b) used latency criteria to separate short-latency reflexive responses to the CS from those that were conditioned or "anticipatory" in nature. Conditioning consisted of ten presentations of a tone (CS), each seven seconds in duration; the UCS was a painful electric shock delivered with the termination of the tone. A CR was defined as a GSR that occurred from four to eight seconds after CS onset, an interval that was not likely to include reflexive GSRs to the CS. Following conditioning, subjects were tested for the degree to which the CR generalized to other stimuli. These generalization stimuli (GS_1 and GS_2) consisted of two tones that differed noticeably from the CS.

The number of CRs given by psychopathic and nonpsychopathic criminals on each trial is plotted in Figure 13. The psychopaths gave fewer CRs than did the nonpsychopaths, and when conditioning did occur they

---

[1] Showed a reduction in the amplitude and/or frequency of CRs when the UCS was no longer presented.

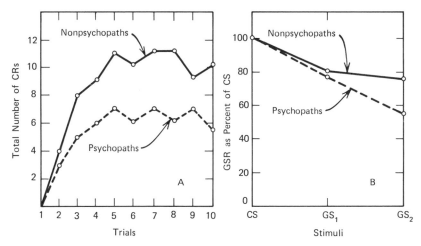

FIGURE 13. Conditioning and generalization of a GSR by psychopathic and nonpsychopathic criminals (after Hare, 1965b).

showed less generalization of the CR to other stimuli than did the nonpsychopaths.

Although the evidence is far from impressive, the studies just reviewed suggest that psychopaths condition poorly when the response is an autonomic one (GSR) but not necessarily when it is a skeletal-muscular one (eyeblink). The discrepancy may be related to the fact that different physiological systems are involved, as well as to the possibility that eyeblink conditioning is influenced by voluntary factors. It is worth noting, in this regard, that the same lack of relationship between eyeblink and GSR conditioning has been found with groups of normal subjects (see, for example, Martin, 1963).

Although it seems that psychopaths do not acquire conditioned GSRs readily, more research is needed in which several autonomic responses are conditioned simultaneously. Since indices of autonomic activity are commonly used to make inferences about the ease and extent to which emotional responses (fear and anxiety) are acquired, both in psychopathic and normal subjects, the use of multiple indices would greatly increase the confidence with which such inferences are made.

INSTRUMENTAL CONDITIONING

So far we have considered the possibility that the psychopath acquires conditioned emotional responses less readily than do other individuals. In the following sections a number of studies dealing with the question of instrumental conditioning and psychopathy is reviewed.

There are several procedural differences between classical and instrumental conditioning (see Kimble, 1961; Melton, 1964). One of the more important distinctions concerns the role of reinforcement and the conditions under which it is administered. In classical conditioning the presentation of the CS and UCS ("reinforcer") is more or less independent of the organism's behavior; it is usually an automatic procedure. In instrumental conditioning, on the other hand, reinforcement depends on an appropriate response from the organism. That is, the organism's behavior is *instrumental* in obtaining reinforcement—the organism must either produce or withhold a response in order to receive reward or avoid punishment. A related but controversial, distinction is that instrumental conditioning usually involves responses that are voluntary in nature, whereas classical conditioning generally involves involuntary behavior.[2]

Avoidance Learning

In his *two-factor theory of avoidance learning,* Mowrer (1947) postulates two stages in learning to avoid punishment. In the first stage cues associated with punishment acquire the capacity to elicit classically conditioned fear responses. The second stage consists of the reinforcement, by fear-reduction, of responses that are instrumental in removing the organism from the fear-producing cues.

The subject can avoid punishment by making some other response (active avoidance) or by inhibiting the punished response (passive avoidance). Concerning the latter, Mowrer (1947) states:

> The performance of any given act normally produces kinesthetic (and often visual, auditory and tactual) stimuli which are perceptible to the performer of the act. If these stimuli are followed a few times by a noxious ("unconditioned") stimulus, they will soon acquire the capacity to produce the emotion of fear. When, therefore, on subsequent occasions the subject starts to perform the previously punished act, the resulting self-stimulation will arouse fear; and the most effective way of eliminating this fear is for the subject to stop the activity which is producing the fear-producing stimuli (p. 136).

The following example should help to clarify the two-factor theory. When a child sees a burning candle for the first time he may reach out to touch the flame. The resulting burn is painful and fear arousing. As the

---

[2] Kimmel (1967) reviewed evidence in support of the contention that autonomic responses, generally considered involuntary, can be instrumentally conditioned. Others (such as Kimble, 1964) feel that the autonomic changes involved in these studies are actually mediated by skeletal-muscular activity.

child begins to reach for the candle on subsequent occasions, the stimuli (for example, sight of the candle and kinesthetic stimuli produced by reaching for the candle) that had previously been present when he was burned, will now elicit conditioned fear-responses. The child can reduce this fear by doing something that removes the fear-arousing stimuli, for example, withdrawing his hand. Since fear reduction is reinforcing, the tendency to avoid touching the burning candle, either by not reaching for it (passive avoidance) or by engaging in some other activity (active avoidance) will be reinforced and strengthened. A considerable amount of research supports this conception of acquired fear as a powerful motivator of behavior (Brown & Farber, 1968).

The relevance of the two-factor theory to psychopathy is that psychopaths appear to have a low capacity for fear conditioning.[3] As a result, they should perform poorly on tasks requiring them to learn to avoid punishment. To test this prediction Lykken (1955) taught psychopathic and neurotic criminals and normal noncriminals an intricate "mental maze." The apparatus was a panel on which there were four levers, a green light, a red light, and a counter labeled "errors." The subject's task was to learn a "maze" that consisted of a sequence of choices among the four levers. There were 20 points of choice, and at each point the machine notified the subject whether he was correct. For a correct response the green light flashed and the machine "moved," with a sound of relays operating, to the next point. At an incorrect response (any of the other three levers) the red light would flash and an error would be recorded on the counter. In addition, one of the three incorrect responses at each point was punished by a strong electric shock. Thus the subject had a two-fold task. The manifest task was to make the correct responses. At the same time the subject could avoid painful punishment by learning to avoid the levers that produced shock. This was the "latent" or hidden task; no mention was made of it to the subject. Each subject was given 20 trials, with the 20-choice sequence the same for each trial.

There were no differences between groups in the rate at which the manifest task was learned, indicating that maze-learning ability per se was similar for each group. In order to obtain a measure of avoidance learning (latent task), the ratio of shocked to unshocked errors was computed for each subject; the lower the ratio the greater the avoidance of shock. The

---

[3] An inference based on the GSR conditioning experiments discussed in the previous section, and on other data considered throughout the rest of this chapter. With respect to GSR conditioning, the conditioned GSRs that occur in experiments using a painful UCS, such as shock, are often considered to be indicative of the extent to which *fear* has been conditioned; such experiments are therefore often referred to as fear-conditioning studies.

results are plotted in Figure 14. It is readily apparent that both the neurotic criminals and the normal noncriminals learned to avoid shock (both groups showed a decreasing avoidance ratio), whereas the psychopaths did not. Moreover, the psychopaths had a significantly higher overall avoidance ratio than did either of the other two groups. Considered in conjunction with the already discussed studies of fear conditionability, Lykken's findings provide support for the hypothesis that psychopathy is related to poor avoidance learning. Additional support for this hypothesis has been provided by several more recent studies (Schachter and Latané, 1964; Schoenherr, 1964; Schmauk, 1968), each of which used electric shock and a "maze" similar to the one just described. In each case, psychopaths did well on the manifest task but not on the avoidance task.

If learning to avoid punishment is dependent on the experience of anticipatory fear, it should be possible to improve a psychopath's performance by somehow augmenting his fear responses. To investigate this possibility, Schachter and Latané (1964) had their subjects learn Lykken's "maze" both with and without an injection of adrenalin, a sympathetic nervous system stimulant. The results without adrenalin were essentially the same as those reported above; that is, psychopaths learned the manifest task but not the latent one of avoiding shocked errors. However, when injected with adrenalin, the psychopaths did very well at avoiding shock. On the assumption that adrenalin-induced sympathetic activity augments the

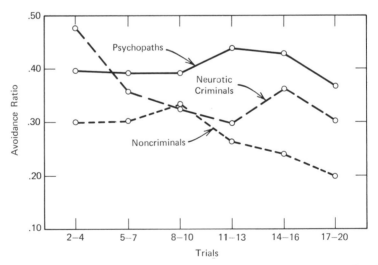

FIGURE 14. Avoidance ratio (shocked errors / nonshocked errors) as a function of trials. A decrease in the avoidance ratio indicates learning to avoid shocked errors (after Lykken, 1955).

experience of fear, these results support the hypothesis that the psychopath's apparent inability to avoid punishment is related to inadequate anticipatory fear responses.

Adrenalin may not be the only way of increasing the psychopath's ability to avoid punishment. It is possible that stronger punishments are needed, since those generally used in these experiments may not really be painful enough either to generate anticipatory fear or to warrant special attempts to avoid them. It is also possible that the use of punishments that are more relevant to the psychopath's value system would be more effective. Schmauk (1968), for example, found that although psychopaths made little attempt to avoid shock or social disapproval, they were quite willing and able to avoid monetary loss.

Anticipation of Punishment

We have suggested that the psychopath's relative inability to avoid punishment is related to the failure of cues associated with punishment to elicit sufficient anticipatory fear for the instigation and subsequent reinforcement of avoidance responses. In a social context, ability to inhibit responses that have previously been punished may be analogous to the concept of conscience or, more specifically, to resistance to temptation. These concepts and their relationship to psychopathy are discussed in Chapter 7. Note that the cues eliciting fear may be symbolic or verbal in nature. For example, the psychopathic person may say to himself, "If I do this, I may get caught and be punished." However, these verbal cues are presumably devoid of the appropriate emotional content, a situation very similar to Cleckley's concept of semantic dementia (see p. 5). To put it another way, the psychopath does not anticipate, in an emotional sense, the unpleasant consequences of his own behavior. In general, the normal individual's anticipation of pain or discomfort is what Freud (1936) referred to as *objective anxiety or fear*—an emotional state triggered by danger signals and characterized by feelings of apprehension and autonomic arousal. According to Freud, a strong anxiety response motivates the individual to remove himself from the source of danger, a conception not unlike Mowrer's two-factor theory (see p. 78). It is obvious that objective anxieties (Freud) or conditioned anticipatory fear responses (Mowrer) have a considerable amount of functional significance for the normal individual.

In this section we consider the suggestion that the degree of apprehension, anxiety, or fear experienced by an individual is inversely related to the remoteness in time of the anticipated pain or discomfort. That is, an aversive event anticipated in the very near future is more fear arousing than a similar event more remote in time (see Figure 15). This hypothesis is based on the assumption that the degree of fear elicited by cues associated with impending or threatened punishment is directly related to the salience of these cues, and that their salience decreases with increased temporal remoteness. There are several reasons for hypothesizing that this *temporal gradient* of fear arousal is steeper for psychopaths than for normal persons. For example, one of the striking things about the psychopath is what has been termed his "short-range hedonism" (Hare, 1965a)—a tendency to satisfy immediate needs even at the risk of experiencing severe discomfort in the future. This suggests that future pain and discomfort are of little immediate consequence to the psychopath. (The psychopath's temporal orientation is discussed in more detail on p. 107). Further, it is possible to conceive of a temporal gradient of fear arousal as a form of stimulus generalization in which the stimulus dimension involved is a temporal one. Since psychopaths show less generalization of a conditioned fear response than do normal persons (Hare, 1965b), by implication, they should also show less temporal generalization. Moreover, as Figure 15 indicates, their temporal gradient of fear arousal should be lower in height than that of other individuals, since their acquired fear responses are relatively small (Lykken, 1955). Some empirical support for these temporal gradients has been provided by several recent studies. In one study (Hare, 1965c), subjects watched consecutive numbers 1 to 12 appear in the window of a memory drum. After this first trial, each subject was told that the series of numbers would be repeated several times and that each time the number 8 appeared he would receive an electric shock equal in intensity to one ear-

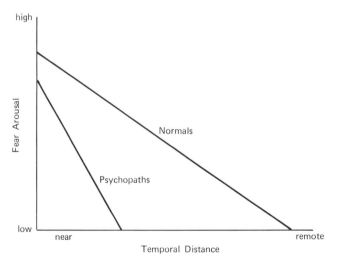

FIGURE 15. Hypothetical relationship between fear arousal and the temporal remoteness of anticipated pain or punishment (after Hare, 1965a).

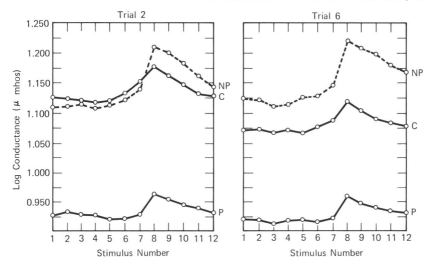

FIGURE 16. Log conductance level as a function of anticipated shock (administered at stimulus number 8). P = psychopathic criminals; NP = nonpsychopathic criminals; C = normal noncriminals (from Hare, 1965c).

lier determined to be the strongest he would tolerate. Skin conductance was monitored throughout the six trials. During the first trial (no shock), all subjects showed a gradual decrease in skin conductance. The results for Trials 2 and 6 (first and last shock trials) are plotted in Figure 16. Compared to the nonpsychopathic criminals (NP) and noncriminal subjects (C), the psychopathic criminals (P) showed very little anticipatory GSR activity prior to the advent of shock. To the extent that skin conductance increases can be considered an indicant of fear arousal, these results suggest that unless the cues are in close temporal proximity to the punishment, they elicit very little fear in the psychopath; that is, the psychopath has a steep temporal gradient of fear arousal.

Somewhat similar results were obtained by Lippert and Senter (1966). Their subjects were told that at the end of a 10-minute period (a clock was visible) they would receive a strong electric shock through electrodes attached to the leg. During the interval the nonpsychopathic subjects showed a considerably greater increase in spontaneous GSR activity than did the psychopathic subjects. Moreover, just before the shock was due, the nonpsychopaths displayed a sharp increase in skin conductance, while none of the psychopaths did so. It is worthwhile noting here that shock was not actually administered at any time during the experiment, so that the results are not due to any group differences in sensitivity to shock. In a recent study, Schalling and Levander (1967) also found that psychopathic delinquents showed less anticipatory spontaneous GSR activity before shock than did anxious delinquents.

The hypothesis that psychopaths have a steeper-than-normal temporal gradient of fear arousal has been incorporated (Hare, 1965a) into a simple model of psychopathy based on Miller's (1959) well-known approach-avoidance theory of behavior. The model is based on the assumption that the tendency to avoid or inhibit a punished response is a function of the degree of conditioned fear elicited by cues associated with the response. Viewed in this way, Figure 15 can also represent the tendency to avoid or inhibit responses as a function of the temporal interval between the response and the anticipated punishment. For instance, all other things being equal, a psychopath would be less likely than would a normal person to inhibit a response, regardless of whether punishment is expected immediately or in the future. It is obvious, of course, that expectation of punishment is not the only factor determining whether some specific behavior will occur. For example, many responses are ambivalent in nature, having both positive (rewarding) and negative (punishing) consequences. In effect, the individual is motivated to make the response and at the same time to inhibit it. Whether the response occurs depends then on the relative weights assigned by the individual to the positive and negative consequences of the response. However, the individual's task is complicated by the fact that the anticipated rewards and punishments are located at different points in time. Thus a response may have immediate rewarding features but delayed unpleasant consequences, and vice versa. The individual's task is therefore one of *temporal integration* (Renner, 1964) in which the relative value or utility of reward and punishment, hence the relative tendency to make or inhibit a response, is a function of their temporal distance from the response.

By combining the gradients in Figure 15 with the postulated temporal reward gradient, we arrive at Figure 17. For the present, the temporal reward gradients (broken line) are assumed to be the same for both psychopaths and normal individuals.[4] With the baseline in Figure 17 representing the estimated time between an action and its consequences, it is evident that if the positive and negative consequences are both expected in the immediate future (for example, at time A), both psychopaths and normal persons would avoid the action, since the tendency to inhibit the response is greater than the tendency to make it. On the other hand, if the positive consequences are expected at time A and the negative consequences at a

---

[4] This assumption is based on the fact that no direct empirical evidence for differential gradients exists. It is likely, however, that the psychopath's temporal gradient of reward is also steeper than that of normal persons. If so, neither reward nor punishments would exist for the psychopath when too far in the future.

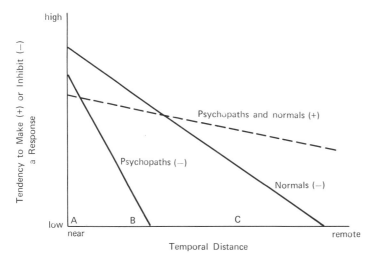

FIGURE 17. The tendency to make or inhibit a response as a function of the temporal remoteness of anticipated reward and punishment (after Hare, 1965a).

later time (for example, at time B), then the normal person, but not the psychopath, would inhibit the response, since the tendency to inhibit the response is greater than the tendency to make it for the normal person but not for the psychopath. Of course, if the negative consequences are very remote (for example, at time C), then even the normal person would make the response. In many ways, this latter situation is analogous with the "live now—pay later" approach to life that seems to be becoming more prevalent in our society.

The model outlined in Figure 17 would predict that deferred payments (negative consequences) and immediate enjoyment (positive consequences) are even more attractive to the psychopath than to the normal person; the psychopath should be (and is) constantly in trouble with credit agencies and finance companies. Moreover, the fact that many psychopaths have a penchant for cashing bad checks and fraudulently obtaining goods is consistent with the model, since immediate rewards more than offset the possible effects of future punishments.[5]

The baseline in Figures 15 and 17 can also be representative of other dimensions, including spatial distance from a goal and similarities between

---

[5] Noting that the psychopath does not experience the sort of anxiety associated with future punishment, Arieti (1967) stated, "He knows theoretically that he may be caught in the antisocial act and be punished. But again, this punishment is a possibility concerning the future and therefore, he does not experience the idea of it with enough emotional strength to change the course of his present actions" (p. 248).

situations and actions. For example, if the baseline in Figure 17 represents similarity between different social situations, we would expect that the effect of punishing the psychopath in one situation would not generalize to other situations unless they were highly similar to the original one. The normal person, on the other hand, would tend to inhibit behavior in a wide variety of situations similar to the one in which the behavior was actually punished. If we assume that the process of socialization involves not only learning to inhibit certain responses but also in the generalization of these inhibitory tendencies to other relevant situations, the model would predict poor socialization in the psychopath.

Although the model is primarily a conditioning one, it is possible to relate it to subcortical mechanisms in the brain. Stein (1964) proposed that it is the anticipation or expectation of rewards and punishments, not their actual occurrence, that motivates behavior. He also argued that the mechanism for reinforcement is a classically conditioned anticipatory response that activates either reward or punishment mechanisms in the hypothalamus, thereby facilitating or inhibiting ongoing behavior. By this token, the psychopath's low capacity for fear (and reward?) conditioning could mean that the expectation of future rewards and punishments does not activate the appropriate subcortical mechanisms and therefore has little effect on his immediate behavior.

Several investigators have found that when faced with unavoidable shock most subjects choose to receive it immediately instead of after a brief delay (Cook and Barnes, 1964; Hare 1966a, 1966b). Most of these subjects reported that waiting for shock to occur was distressing and that it was better to get it over with as soon as possible. There is also some evidence that when it does come the delayed shock is subjectively more intense than an immediate one (Hare and Petrusic, 1967), probably because the emotional arousal associated with waiting for the shock enhances the experience of pain (Melzack and Wall, 1965). If the preference for an immediate punishment is based on the fear associated with waiting for the punishment to occur, we might expect the psychopath to show more of a preference for delayed shock than do nonpsychopaths. To test this prediction, psychopathic and nonpsychopathic subjects were given six trials on which to choose between receiving a strong electric shock either immediately or after a 10-second delay (Hare, 1966a). Psychopathic criminals chose immediate shock 55.5 percent of the time, while nonpsychopathic criminals and normal noncriminals chose it 87.5 percent and 78.9 percent of the time, respectively. All of the 31 nonpsychopathic subjects chose the immediate shock on at least four out of the six trials, while only five of the twelve psychopaths chose immediate shock four or more times. A better picture of the data is obtained by considering the percentage of immedi-

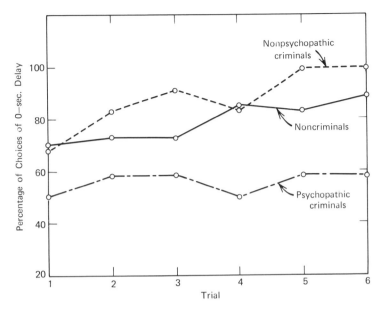

FIGURE 18. Percentage of choices of the immediate shock during each trial (after Hare, 1966a).

ate-shock choices on a trial-by-trial basis. As Figure 18 indicates, the choices of the psychopaths remained more or less constant, while those of the other groups increased in the direction of greater preference for immediate shock. These results can be interpreted in terms of a conditioned-fear hypothesis. That is, cues associated with painful stimulation are classically conditioned to elicit fear responses in the interval prior to anticipated pain. (Presumably, the aversive properties of this aroused fear combined with those of delayed shock are greater than the aversive properties of immediate shock alone.) Since the aroused fear is a conditioned response, its magnitude should increase with repeated shock experiences, and this should be reflected in an increased number of choices of immediate shock over trials. As Figure 18 indicates, this is what happened in the case of the nonpsychopathic subjects. Similarly, the fact that psychopaths acquire conditioned fear responses poorly suggests that even after a number of shock experiences relatively little fear would be generated by cues preceding delayed shock. This would account for the failure of the psychopaths to show an increased number of immediate shock choices over trials.

Verbal Conditioning

A vast literature on the instrumental conditioning of verbal behavior has accumulated during the last 15 years (see review by Kanfer, 1968).

Since these studies involve the use of rewards and punishments in a social context, it is understandable that they would be extended to the study of psychopathy, in which some form of social malfunction seems to be evident.

Most studies of psychopathy have used a simple procedure in which the subject is presented with a series of index cards, each containing a commonly used past-tense verb (for example, ran, worked) and a number of pronouns (for example, I, we, he, they). The subject is shown the cards one at a time with the instructions to make up a sentence beginning with one of the pronouns and incorporating the verb printed on the card. Sentences that begin with certain pronouns (usually "I" or "we") are either rewarded (the experimenter says "good," "mm-hmm," or so on) or punished (the experimenter says "wrong," "uh-uh," or so forth). Verbal conditioning is considered to have occurred when the increase in the frequency of the reinforced response class is greater than that shown by other subjects who have not received reinforcement.

The verbal conditioning studies of psychopathy have provided little support for the hypotheses that psychopaths are unable to learn socially reinforced responses. Some investigators (Johns and Quay, 1962; Quay and Hunt, 1965) have reported that psychopathic criminals do not condition as well as do neurotic criminals; however, their data were not very convincing. Other investigators (Blaylock, 1960; Bryan and Kapche, 1967) have found that psychopaths condition as well as do other subjects. One study (Bernard and Eisenman, 1967) found that female psychopaths conditioned *better* than did a group of nurses. In this study the reinforcements were administered by a male experimenter, which led the authors to suggest that the great effectiveness of social reinforcement may have been related to the fact that the female psychopaths had been separated from men for some time and were therefore highly motivated to receive praise from the male experimenter.

The results of these studies can be better understood when it is realized that verbal conditioning involves a complex social interaction between the subject and experimenter. Whether conditioning occurs (in the form of an increase in reinforced responses) depends on a number of variables, including the subject's awareness of the response-reinforcement contingency and his motivation to receive the reinforcement offered. Conditioning is inferred from changes in the number of reinforced responses; but failure to observe such a change does not necessarily mean that the subject has not learned the response-reinforcement relationship. He may be perfectly aware of what he is supposed to do to make the experimenter say "good," but for a variety of reasons chooses not to cooperate. This means that even if a group of psychopaths does not show an increase in the frequency of reinforced responses, we cannot conclude that they have not learned what they are supposed to do. They simply may not be motivated enough to make use of what they have learned. It would be useful if subsequent verbal-conditioning studies of psychopathy made some attempt to assess awareness of the response-reinforcement contingency, attitude towards the experimenter, motivation to receive reinforcement, and so on.

PROBABILITY LEARNING

In the studies just discussed the relationship between the subject's behavior and its consequences was simple and generally easy to learn. That is, the subject made a response and received more or less immediate reinforcement or feedback. A logical question to ask at this point is how well the psychopath would perform on tasks in which the temporal interval between his behavior and the resulting consequences is relatively great, or the relationship between behavior and consequences uncertain. Although no pertinent research on this question has as yet been published, we might expect that the psychopath would do rather poorly when what he does *now* is determined by what may happen *in the future* (see Figure 15). A related question concerns the extent to which the psychopath is able to learn or perceive the relationship between past events and the consequences of his present actions.

A study by Painting (1961) bears on this latter question. The subjects in this *probability learning* experiment were psychopathic and neurotic criminals and a group of college students comparable in intelligence to the two criminal groups. Briefly, the subject was required to predict which of two lights (right or left) would come on during each of 200 trials. Some subjects were rewarded with cigarettes for making correct predictions or responses, while other subjects were punished with the loss of cigarettes for incorrect responses. Three different sequences were involved. In one sequence, the correct response was randomly determined, that is, it was independent of what had taken place on earlier trials. During this sequence, the psychopaths tended to repeat the response that had been correct on the immediately preceding trial, a strategy that Painting referred to as rigid and stereotyped, but that could also involve "going along with a winner" or avoiding the "gambler's fallacy."

In the second sequence the correct response on any given trial was dependent on the immediately preceding trial. If a particular response had been correct on the preceding trial, there was a 75 percent chance that it would be incorrect on the subsequent trial. The subject's best strategy, therefore, would be to choose the response that was incorrect on the preceding trial. Under these conditions, the psychopaths did somewhat better than did the subjects in the other two groups.

In the third sequence the correct response on any given trial was dependent only on what had happened *two* trials earlier. The correct response on any given trial was opposite to that which had been correct two trials earlier. On this rather complex sequence, the performance of the psychopaths deteriorated compared to that of the other subjects, indicating, perhaps, that psychopaths have difficulty in perceiving the relationships or contingencies between past events and the consequences of their present behavior. Adequate social functioning is no doubt partly dependent on the perception of these contingencies and also on a willingness to be guided by them. Although it is possible that psychopaths have difficulty in discovering such contingencies, it is also possible that their real deficiency is in not being sufficiently motivated to be guided by this knowledge.

ROTE VERBAL LEARNING

A prodigious amount of research has been concerned with the processes and variables involved in the rote learning of verbal material (see Jung, 1968). The use of psychopathic subjects in these studies is based on several considerations. In the first place, the results of such studies are relevant to the question of whether psychopathy is related to the learning and retention of verbal material. Second, the use of psychopaths as subjects provides a means of testing various hypotheses about the effects of anxiety on learning and performance.

The most popular paradigms are *serial learning* and *paired-associates learning*. In serial learning a subject is presented with a list of verbal items, usually nonsense syllables (for example, BEW, JIV), and is required to learn them in the order presented. In paired-associates learning a subject is presented with pairs of items (for example, GEX-MIP) and is required to recall the second (or response) member of the pair (that is, MIP) when presented with the first, or stimulus member (that is, GEX). In spite of the fact that the functional stimuli are easier to identify and the processes probably better understood in paired-associates learning, all the relevant studies of psychopathy have, for some reason or other, used serial learning tasks.

In an early study, Fairweather (1953) found that psychopathic and neurotic criminals learned a list of 10 nonsense syllables more slowly than did a group of "normal" criminals. When cigarettes were used as incentives, the performance of all three groups improved, although the normal group was still somewhat superior to the other two groups. Several other studies, however, have failed to find any significant differences in serial learning between psychopathic and other criminals, either with incentives (Kadlub, 1956) or without them (Schoper, 1958). Similar results were obtained by Hetherington and Klinger (1964), although in this case the subjects were college students with high and low scores on the MMPI *Pd* scale (see p. 16). An additional finding in this study was that critical, disparaging remarks by the experimenter disrupted the performance of the low-*Pd* subjects but had no effect on the high-*Pd* ones. Whether similar results would be obtained with diagnosed psychopaths is unknown; in any case, the results of the Hetherington and Klinger study are suggestive and certainly consistent with the general belief that psychopaths are relatively impervious to social criticism.

Several investigators have used serial learning tasks to test the clinical impression that psychopaths have excellent memories (Pennington, 1954). The paradigm used is based on the fact that one of the important determinants of forgetting is *retroactive inhibition*—the interference of "new" learning with the retention of "old" learning (see Jung, 1968). In this retroaction design a subject learns a serial list of items (task *A*), then learns another list (task *B*), and is finally tested for retention of the material learned in task *A;* his retention scores are compared to those of other subjects who have not had task *B* interpolated between task *A* and the subsequent test for retention.

Sherman (1957) used the retroaction design with psychopathic and normal criminals and a noncriminal group of psychoneurotic patients. For half the subjects tasks *A* and *B* consisted of two different lists of nonsense syllables; for the other half, the items were common words. The procedure for all three groups was: Learn task *A*, learn task *B*, relearn task *A*. Retention was determined by the number of items correctly recalled on the first trial of relearning task *A* (recall) and by the number of trials taken to relearn task *A* (savings). On both measures of retention and with both types of verbal material, the psychopaths performed best and the neurotics worst. However, a subsequent study by Schoper (1958), using similar subjects and procedures, failed to support Sherman's findings. The experimental evidence concerning superior memory and retention in psychopaths is therefore equivocal at best.

Many of the comments made earlier about verbal conditioning are applicable to rote learning. Any differences in the performance of psychopaths and normal subjects probably has more to do with motivational factors than with differences in the capacity to learn.

PSYCHOPATHY, ANXIETY, AND LEARNING

We have seen that the psychopath's comparative failure to avoid punishment can be interpreted in terms of insufficient conditioned anxiety. In general, we expect him to do poorly in situations in which good performance is at least partially dependent on the reinforcing effects of anxiety-reduction.

There are other situations, however, in which the effect of anxiety is more dependent on whether it elicits responses that are relevant to the task at hand or responses that are incompatible with the task (task-irrelevant). This conception of anxiety is based on Spence's theory of emotionally based drive and its relationship to aversive conditioning (Spence and Spence, 1966). In this theory *the tendency to make a response* (E), is a multiplicative function of a learning factor or *habit strength* (H) and *generalized drive* (D); in other words, $E = f(H \times D)$. Drive level is dependent on the intensity of noxious stimulation involved and on the extent to which conditioned stimuli elicit internal emotional or anxiety responses. The theory predicts that a high level of anxiety (high D) will facilitate performance in classical aversive conditioning. In this respect the psychopath's poor GSR conditioning is seen to be related to a low level of anxiety (hence drive).

When more complex learning tasks are involved, however, the effect of anxiety depends on the number and strength of the competing responses present. A high level of anxiety should facilitate performance *only* when the initial strength of the correct to-be-learned response is greater than that of the incorrect, competing responses; it should *retard* performance when the correct response is initially weaker than the incorrect responses.[6] In other words, all other things being equal, the psychopath (with his low level of anxiety) should perform poorly on some tasks and very well on others. As an example, the degree of response competition in serial rote-learning tasks can be increased by increasing the similarity between items. When intralist similarity (hence intralist competition) is low—a kind of task facilitated by anxiety—a psychopath should not perform as well as a normal person. On the other hand, if the task involves a high degree of in-

---

[6] Broverman et al. (1968) have reviewed a considerable amount of empirical evidence that relates performance to the relative degree of adrenergic and cholinergic activity and that is consistent with the Spences' analysis. Briefly, adrenergic (SNS) stimulation improves performance on classical conditioning and simple perceptual-motor tasks. However, an increase in adrenergic activity impairs performance of tasks that require the inhibition or delay of otherwise prepotent responses.

tralist similarity (for example, DAX, DEX, PEX), a psychopath should perform better than more anxious individuals, since in this case anxiety increases the probability that competing responses will be elicited, interfering with the task. It follows that on tasks involving some intermediate degree of response competition a psychopath should perform about as well as a normal person.

Spence and Spence (1966) have extended the theory of emotionally based drive to include situations in which drive- or anxiety-related stimuli elicit task-irrelevant responses. This extension, termed the response-interference hypothesis, states that task-irrelevant responses, which in some situations may interfere with efficient performance, are more easily elicited in anxious than in nonanxious subjects. Among the task-irrelevant responses assumed to be elicited during heightened states of anxiety are autonomic reactions and covert verbalizations reflecting self-depreciation, anger, desire to escape, and so on. Since these responses are most likely to occur under conditions of psychological or physical stress (ego-involving instructions, fear of failure, noxious stimulation, and so forth), we might expect that the introduction of stress into a learning situation would lead to less of a performance decrement in psychopaths than in other subjects. The results of the Hetherington and Klinger (1964) study discussed earlier (p. 91) might be interpreted in this way.

Note that this discussion of the effects of anxiety on performance is based on the assumption that all other things are equal. It is obvious that the effects of anxiety may be all but washed out by a host of cognitive, attitudinal, and motivational variables associated with psychopathy and not under direct experimental control. Nevertheless, it would be worthwhile to determine whether the psychopath actually does perform complex tasks more efficiently under stress than do other individuals. A related problem would be to investigate the conditions that actually generate stress in the psychopath.

SUMMARY

The evidence discussed in this chapter permits several tentative conclusions to be drawn.

It appears that psychopaths do not develop conditioned fear responses readily. As a result, they find it difficult to learn responses that are motivated by fear and reinforced by fear reduction. The fact that their behavior appears to be neither motivated nor guided by the possibility of unpleasant consequences, particularly when the temporal relationship between behavior and its consequences is relatively great, might be interpreted in this way.

There is some evidence that psychopaths are also less influenced than are normal persons by the relationship between past events and the consequences of their present behavior.

Psychopaths perform well on verbal conditioning and rote-learning tasks, as well as on tasks that are not dependent on acquired fear. Any differences between their performance and that of normal persons on these tasks probably result from a lack of motivation and from the use of inappropriate incentives instead of from an inability to learn the task. Several considerations lead to the prediction that when these tasks are complex, involving many competing responses, or when they must be performed under stressful conditions, psychopaths may actually perform them better than would normal individuals.

CHAPTER SEVEN

PSYCHOPATHY
AND SOCIALIZATION

PARENTAL CORRELATES OF PSYCHOPATHY

Perhaps the most popular generalization about psychopathy is that it is related to some form of early disturbance in family relationships, including parental loss, emotional deprivation, parental rejection, and inconsistent disciplinary techniques. For instance, a review of the research literature led Gregory (1958) to conclude that there were indications of a high incidence of parental loss in individuals who later became psychopathic or antisocial. A study by Greer (1964) supported this conclusion; 60 percent of 79 psychopaths studied had experienced parental loss, although only 28 percent of 387 neurotics and 27 percent of 691 normal subjects had experienced a similar loss. Moreover, the psychopaths experienced parental loss at an earlier age (the majority before age five) than did the other subjects. Related evidence suggests that the more severe the psychopathic behavior is, the more likely it is that there was parental deprivation (Craft, Stephenson, and Granger, 1964). However, a study by Oltman and Friedman (1967) indicates that the type of parental deprivation involved must be taken into account. The results of this extensive study are summarized in Table 6. Although the differences between some conditions where not especially large, it is noteworthy that the differences that did exist were restricted to parental loss by separation. Moreover, additional data not included in Table 6 indicate that, compared to the other subjects, psychopaths were much more likely to have been separated from their fathers than from their mothers. If only those psychopaths who had been institutionalized before the age of 19 are considered, 65 percent (of 101) had experienced parental loss, 17.8 percent by death and 47.5 percent by separation. Over half of these separations involved the father. Since separation from the parents was more closely related to psychopathy than were other forms of parental loss, Oltman and Friedman suggested that parental deprivation per se is of less importance in producing psychopathy than are the emotional and physical disturbances that probably preceded the physical departure of the parents.

> It may well be presumed, at least in many instances, that the departing parent has already created a difficult psychological and emotional atmosphere in the home. Separation and/or divorce of parents is usually the result of conflicts and difficulties which undoubtedly have traumatized the child prior to the parent's physical departure. The parent (usually the father) who deserts his family is presumptively unstable, irresponsible, and heedless of the children. He may be alcoholic, physically abusive, promiscuous, shiftless. Is it not credible that the impact of these factors upon the child exerts an adverse influence equal to, or greater than, the physical absence of the parent? (Oltman and Friedman, 1967, pp. 302–303).

Several other investigators have also suggested that disturbances in the parent-child relationship may lead to psychopathy. After surveying the literature, for example, McCord and McCord (1964) concluded that emo-

TABLE 6: Incidence and Type of Parental Loss as a Function of Psychiatric Classification (After Oltman and Friedman, 1967.)

Group	N	Type of Parental Loss (%)			
		Death	Separation	Mental Illness	Total
Psychopaths	301	20.6	27.9	0.7	49.2
Drug addicts	69	23.2	20.3	0	43.5
Psychoneuroses	363	25.3	14.9	0.3	40.5
Alcoholic states	1103	29.3	7.9	0.6	37.9
Organic conditions	341	22.9	11.4	2.3	36.7
Neurotic depressions	377	20.4	13.5	1.3	35.3
Schizophrenia	2921	23.4	8.9	2.8	35.0
Affective psychoses	829	23.9	7.1	2.4	33.4
Normal subjects	350	26.9	7.4	0	34.3

tional deprivation or severe parental rejection is one of the main causes of psychopathy. They also concluded that mild rejection, in combination with (1) brain damage or (2) a psychopathic parent, erratically punitive discipline, or absence of adult supervision, can produce psychopathy. Similarly, on the basis of an extensive study of guidance clinic cases, Jenkins (1966) suggested that the unsocialized aggressive (psychopathic) child had experienced general and continual parental (especially maternal) rejection. Further, there was evidence that the mothers of these children were themselves emotionally unstable.

Several studies have found that antisocial and delinquent behavior are related to erratic and inconsistent disciplinary and socialization techniques on behalf of the parents (Andry, 1960; Bennet, 1960; McCord and McCord, 1964). Whether a similar relationship exists between psychopathy and inconsistency is not known, although a study by Robins (1966), discussed on p. 98, indicates that inadequate parental discipline may be a factor in psychopathic behavior.

Not everyone agrees that psychopaths tend to come from broken homes or that they have experienced some form of parental loss or rejection. Cleckley (1964), for example, commented that "During all my years of experience with hundreds of psychopaths . . . no type of parent or of parental influence, overt or subtle, has been regularly demonstrable" (p. 452). He further noted that a very large percentage of his psychopathic patients came from backgrounds that appeared to be conducive to "happy development and excellent adjustment." One of the reasons for these discrepant findings may be the fact that Cleckley's patients were largely from middle-class backgrounds where disturbed parent-child relationships may be more subtle and less likely to come to the attention of social agencies and investigators than are similar disturbances that occur in the lower-class family environments.

Another reason for being cautious about accepting the parental rejection and inconsistent socialization interpretations of psychopathy is that most of the persons who come from what appear to be similarly disturbed backgrounds do not become psychopaths. Inconsistent socialization practices, for example, are related to a wide spectrum of later disturbances, including psychopathy and many forms of delinquent, neurotic, and psychotic behavior (Wiggins, 1968). Clearly, the gross type of disturbed family relationships generally discussed by most investigators are neither necessary nor sufficient conditions for the development of psychopathy.

A major limitation of the studies discussed so far is that they have used a retroactive approach; that is, information about early family experiences has been obtained either from the adult psychopath himself or from his parents, relatives, and friends, all of whom may be understandably reluctant (or unable) to recall reliably what society would consider to be inadequate child-rearing practices. A study by Robins and her associates did not have this limitation, and because of its thoroughness and scope provides the most extensive data available on the sociological development of psychopathy.

The study, summarized by Robins (1966), described the adult social and psychiatric status of 524 persons who had been referred to a psychiatric clinic some 30 years earlier, between 1924 and 1929. Of these, 406 had been referred for antisocial behavior and 118 for a variety of other behavior disorders. Besides the clinical referrals, 100 normal control subjects were followed up and studied. Many of the subjects that had been clinic referrals in childhood became psychiatrically disturbed adults. About 22 percent of the clinic referrals and only 2 percent of the normal controls received an adult diagnosis of sociopathic personality (psychopathy).

The childhood predictors of adult psychopathy were summarized as follows:

> If one wishes to choose the most likely candidate for a later diagnosis of sociopathic personality from among children appearing in a child guidance clinic, the best choice appears to be the boy referred for theft or aggression who has shown a diversity of antisocial behavior in many episodes, at least one of which could be grounds for a Juvenile Court appearance, and whose antisocial behavior involves him with strangers and organizations as well as with teachers and parents. With these characteristics, more than half of the boys appearing at the clinic were later diagnosed sociopathic personality. Such boys had a history of truancy, theft, staying out late, and refusing to obey parents. They lied gratuitously, and showed little guilt over their behavior. They were generally irresponsible about being where they were supposed to be or taking care of money. They were interested in sexual activities and had experimented with homosexual relationships. . . . (Robins, 1966, p. 157).

TABLE 7: Childhood and Family Characteristics of Sociopaths and Other Patients (After Robins, 1966.)

Characteristics	Percentage of Sociopaths (N = 94)	Percentage of Other Patients (N = 342)
Male	85	70
Referred for any antisocial behavior	95	66
For theft	40	20
For sexual problems (girls only)	29	11

Characteristics	Percentage of Sociopaths (N = 94)	Percentage of Other Patients (N = 342)
Symptoms		
Theft	81	49
Incorrigible	79	52
Running away	71	39
Truancy	66	36
Bad companions	56	36
Sexual activity and excessive interest		
(Boys)	56	44
(Girls)	79	62
Stay out late	55	35
School discipline problems	53	31
Aggressive	45	26
Reckless	35	23
Impulsive	38	20
Slovenly	32	17
Enuretic	32	21
Lack guilt	32	14
Lying without cause	26	11
Median age at referral	(14)[a]	(13)[a]
Median age of onset	(7)[a]	(7)[a]
Girls only	(13)[a]	(8)[a]
Juvenile court case	79	39
Sent to correctional institution	51	17
School retardation at referral	68	55
Final school level, eighth-grade graduate	62	36
Antisocial toward		
Parents	73	50
Teachers and other authority figures	83	57
Strangers	39	21
Businesses	41	20
Family patterns		
Father sociopathic or alcoholic	53	32
Broken home, all causes	67	63
Divorce and separation	44	33
Impoverished home	55	38
Patient is only child	18	14
Patient is 1 of 4 children	27	17

[a] Numbers are ages, not percentages.

Girls likely to be diagnosed psychopathic as adults were similar to the boys except that they were more frequently involved in sexual misbehaviors.

These childhood characteristics, along with data on family background, are summarized in Table 7. Concerning family backgrounds, it is evident that most of the psychopaths, as well as the other patients, came from homes that were impoverished and broken by divorce and separation. However, most of the psychopaths also had fathers who were either psychopathic or alcoholic; separation from the father at an early age did not lessen the chances that the child would develop into an adult psychopath. The importance of the father's behavior in predicting similar antisocial behavior in his offspring, whether male or female, is consistent with the results of several recent studies, which found that maternal rejection and maternal behavior have less to do with the development of delinquency than do the personality and behavior of the father (Andry, 1957; Marcus, 1960).

Robins notes that the consequences of having an antisocial father include a lack of adequate discipline in the home and a family life characterized by parental discord. When discipline is adequate or strict and parental discord absent, the tendency for an antisocial father to have a child who is later diagnosed psychopathic is considerably decreased. An interesting point here is that cold, unaffectionate fathers tended to have *fewer* psychopathic children—an unexpected finding that Robins suggested was related to the fact that such fathers were usually strict disciplinarians; as already noted, strict discipline tended to decrease the incidence of adult psychopathy.

Unlike the investigators discussed earlier in this chapter. Robins did not find that parental loss or rejection were, in themselves, related to psychopathy. She found, as Oltman and Friedman (1967) have also suggested, that the circumstances surrounding parental loss and rejection were the important factors.

> The relation between broken or discordant homes and delinquency or adult criminality so often interpreted in the literature as showing that broken homes "cause" delinquency or criminality may well be a spurious relationship occuring only because having an antisocial father simultaneously produces adult antisocial behavior in the children and marital discord between the parents (Robins, 1966, p. 179).

Similarly, rejection of the child generally occurred either because the parents were irresponsible or because the child's behavior was intolerable, or both. This interactive relationship between the behavior of parents and child is in keeping with the current thinking (see, for example, Bell, 1968;

Kagan, 1968) that most models of socialization are unidirectional and hence incomplete. Bell (1968) argued that the behavior of the parent toward the child is largely influenced by the characteristics of the child (including genetic and congenital features) and by the *upper and lower limits* that the parents place on their child's behavior. For example, on the assumption that there are congenital determinants of assertiveness, the usual finding that excessive use of physical punishment is related to delinquency could be interpreted to mean not that the punishment produced delinquency (perhaps by inducing frustration or by providing a model for aggressive behavior), but instead that the congenital assertiveness of the child activated parental control in the form of physical punishment and restraint. Similarly, moral development, usually interpreted as the outcome of parental affection and discipline, may also be related to genetic differences in what has been variously called *person orientation* (Bell, 1968), *social attachment* (Schaffer and Emerson, 1964), *social responsiveness* (Scarr, 1965), and *extraversion-introversion* (Eysenck, 1964; Gottesman, 1966). Bell (1968) suggested, for example, that children showing little internalization of a moral orientation may have been congenitally low in person orientation, that is, that they were less attentive to and influenced by the behavior and needs of others, with the result that their mothers were less affectionate and did not appeal to the child's personal or social values.

With respect to the relationship between inconsistent socialization and later psychological and behavioral disturbance, Wiggins (1968) noted that the child's maladaptive behavior may produce or augment inconsistency on the part of the parents. In an attempt to deal with a difficult child the parents may try various disciplinary techniques, shifting back and forth between overindulgence and a harsh, punitive regimen. It is also possible that the ". . . parents' inconsistent socialization practices . . . represent both a cause and an effect of the child's maladaptive behavior, the parental and child behaviors reciprocally augmenting one another to culminate in a vicious spiral" (Wiggins, 1968, p. 325).

The point here is that psychopathy may very well represent the outcome of interactions between the characteristics (possibly congenital) of the child and the socialization techniques employed.

SOME SOCIALIZATION THEORIES OF PSYCHOPATHY

Role-Taking Ability

Gough (1948) has outlined a theory of psychopathy based on the concept of role-playing. Role-playing involves putting oneself in another's shoes, trying to see oneself as others do. Socialization, cooperation, and self-control are all considered to be dependent on the appropriate role-taking experiences, since such experiences permit an individual to predict in advance how others will behave and how they will react to his own behavior. Gough assumes that the psychopath is pathologically deficient in the ability to role-play. As a consequence, he is unable to regard himself as a social object and to foresee the social consequences of his own behavior; and because he cannot judge his own behavior from another's point of view, he is unable to experience embarrassment, loyalty, contrition, or group identification. He cannot understand the reasons for society's objections to his behavior nor the punishment meted out by it. He is inconsiderate of the wishes and needs of others, lacks inhibitions, and forms no deep attachments because he cannot identify with others.

Some indirect support for Gough's theory comes from a study by Reed and Cuadra (1957). Student nurses were asked to describe themselves, describe others in the group, and predict how the others would describe them. Subjects who scored high on a scale related to psychopathy were less successful in predicting how others would describe them than were those with low scores on the scale. Moreover, the former were rated by their peers as being less insightful than the latter. An insightful person, in this case, was defined as one who has the ". . . ability to recognize and understand the motives underlying her behavior and is aware of the effects of her behavior on other persons [and who] is alert to what other people think of her as a person" (Reed and Cuadra, 1957, p. 388). Several studies discussed in the last chapter are at least consistent with Gough's role-taking theory.

Unfortunately, Gough does not indicate why psychopaths should be deficient in role-taking. One possibility, discussed earlier (p. 49), is that they are unable to construct the "emotional facsimiles" required for empathy with others. A related possibility is that they may be congenitally low in person orientation (see Bell, 1968), with the result that little of their behavior is oriented toward and influenced by others. Another possible reason for defective role-playing is based on Greenacre's (1945) suggestion that psychopathy is the result of having a stern, remote father (but see the reference to Robins' study on p. 100) and an indulgent, pleasure-loving, and frivolous mother, both parents being narcissistic and overly dependent on external appearances. The child adopts a kind of "show-window display" role in which behavior that reflects favorably on the parents is rewarded and failures on the part of the child are denied, concealed, or explained away. As a result, the child is

> . . . robbed of the full measure of reality testing, and performance even in
> the earliest years becomes measured by its appearance rather than by its in-

trinsic accomplishment. One sees in miniature the attitudes which later are so characteristic of the psychopath, i.e., what *seems* to be is more valued than what *is*. This characteristic, together with the essential emotional impoverishment, tends to create a very thin stage-property vision of reality in which the facade at any given time is the prime consideration (Greenacre, 1945, p. 449).

The suggestion that psychopaths may learn a social facade with no moral or emotional constraints other than what "looks good to others" at the time is reminiscent of Cleckley's concept of semantic dementia. If there are no "real" reasons for socially acceptable behavior, then the psychopath's surprise at society's demands of him is understandable. Indeed, it will be recalled that the *complex* psychopath, according to Arieti (1967), is one who appears to operate exclusively on what is or is not socially acceptable from a rational point of view instead of from an emotional one. Thus, although he may behave acceptably in some ways, when seeking release from tension he may be surprised that he is criticized for doing what appeared to him to be logical and acceptable under the circumstances.

Conscience Development and Psychopathy

Although several psychodynamic interpretations have been made of the psychopath's presumably inadequate conscience (see, for example, Greenacre, 1945), the present section is devoted to learning theory models of conscience development.[1] A model outlined by Solomon and his associates (Solomon, 1960; Solomon, Turner, and Lessac, 1968) seems particularly relevant to psychopathy.

Solomon assumes that what is usually called "conscience" may be thought of as being comprised of two partially independent components: *resistance to temptation* and *guilt*. The differentiation and genesis of these components are well illustrated in experiments in which dogs learned to avoid punishment by choosing the less preferable of two foods—dry dog chow instead of meat. Briefly, dogs that were punished early in the response sequence, as they approached the "tabooed" meat, showed greater resistance to temptation on later tests, and less signs of emotional disturbance (guilt), than did dogs who were punished after they had been allowed to eat some of the meat. These latter dogs, while showing little resistance to temptation—they readily went back to eating the tabooed meat as soon as the experimenter was absent from the room—exhibited signs of emotional disturbance after making the transgression. An interesting finding in early studies (Solomon, 1960) was that there were species differences in

---

[1] For an extensive discussion of the socialization processes involved in the development of conscience and internalized control of behavior, the reader is referred to Aronfreed (1968).

the ease with which temptation was resisted. Dogs that were timid in approaching humans and that were easily frightened by loud noises (such as Shetland sheepdogs) learned very quickly to resist eating the tabooed meat. "On the other hand, Basenjis seem to be constitutional psychopaths and it is very difficult to maintain taboos in such dogs" (p. 402). The reason for these differences in ability to resist temptation may be related to differences in fear conditionability.

We have already seen (p. 78) that some investigators assume that the major effect of punishment is to permit the conditioning of fear to stimuli, including proprioceptive stimuli, that immediately precede punishment. Inhibition of the response is then reinforced through fear-reduction. In other words, punishment early in a response sequence should be very effective at producing response inhibition (resistance to temptation) and little guilt since the stimuli that elicit fear occur early enough in the sequence to disrupt it, whereas punishment administered later in the sequence should result in low resistance to temptation but a large amount of guilt. A diagram of these relationships is presented in Figure 19. However, since psychopaths do not acquire conditioned fear responses readily, we might expect them to experience little guilt and to be low in resistance to temptation (similar to the Basenjis), even when punishment occurs early in the sequence.

An interpretation that does not depend on assumptions about the psychopath's low capacity for fear conditioning is also possible. We might assume that psychopaths are individuals who, as children, were punished for their transgressions relatively late in the response sequence. For example, the child may steal a cookie and not be punished either until he begins eating it (point *C* in Figure 19) or sometime after he has eaten it (point *D*).

Response Sequence

	A	*B*	*C*	*D*
Stimulus (Cookie Jar) ⟶	Approaches Jar	Takes Cookie	Eats Cookie	Sometime Later
	Punishment here results in: (1) High resistance to temptation (2) Low guilt	Punishment here results in: (1) Low resistance to temptation (2) High guilt	Punishment here results in: (1) Low resistance to temptation (2) Low guilt	

FIGURE 19. **Hypothetical relationship between delay of punishment, resistance to temptation, and guilt (based on Solomon, 1960 and Solomon et al., 1968).**

According to Solomon's model, punishment at point *C* should produce low resistance to temptation and a large amount of guilt. This may seem somewhat contradictory, but it is worth noting that many clinicians are convinced that some psychopaths do experience guilt over their transgressions. Even if they do, Solomon's research indicates that guilt does not necessarily generate resistance to temptation. In some respects, of course, the consequences of being punished at point *C* are more descriptive of the neurotic delinquent than of the psychopath.

Although Solomon has not discussed the case when punishment is received well after the response sequence has been completed (at point *D*), or not received at all, we might predict that this would result in low resistance to temptation and low guilt, since all of the stimuli related to the response sequence are well removed from the punishment. The person who shows low resistance to temptation and low guilt is, of course, the psychopath, and we might therefore hypothesize that psychopathy is partially the result of punishment that is considerably delayed and perhaps administered inconsistently. For instance, the child takes a tabooed cookie and his mother says that he's "going to get it" when his father comes home; meanwhile the child eats the cookie and when father gets home hours later he is spanked, but the child does not connect the spanking with the earlier cookie-stealing episode, except, perhaps, on a vague verbal level. Or, as Maher (1966) suggested, the child may be able to forestall punishment by suitable expressions of repentance and promises not to repeat the behavior, with the result that repentance behavior is reinforced and the fear of punishment associated with forbidden acts extinguished. Even if punishment is administered, it may be so inconsistent as to be ineffective, or it may be arbitrary and unrelated to a specific deviant act.

An interesting point here is that Solomon et al. (1968) suggested that not only does delayed punishment lead to low resistance to temptation, but also that in somewhat different situations resistance to temptation is even less. That is, inhibitory responses acquired under delayed punishment and in a particular environment do not generalize to other, different environments. In other words, if the child-rearing experiences of psychopaths were characterized by delayed or inconsistent punishment, whatever inhibitory responses they acquired in one situation would not generalize to other situations. Recall that, although based on different premises, essentially the same point was made in Chapter 6 (see especially Figures 13 and 15).

If we assume that psychopaths do not acquire conditioned fear responses readily (perhaps for congenital reasons), then it would follow that the timing of punishment for these individuals would be even more crucial than it would be for other persons. That is, for punishment to have any effect at all in producing resistance to temptation in psychopaths, it would have to occur reliably at some optimal point in the response sequence. The combination of poor fear conditionability and inefficient punishment techniques could therefore be important determinants of psychopathy.

In some respects, Solomon's analysis of conscience is similar to the conceptualization of morality outlined by Brown (1965). According to Brown, the dimensions of morality are knowledge, feelings, and conduct. Moral knowledge, or awareness of the rules of society, is acquired through the processes of concept formation and cognitive learning; moral feelings, including guilt, shame, and remorse, are the product of classical conditioning; and moral behavior, being dependent on knowledge and feelings, is governed by the principles of instrumental and imitative learning. The significance of this conception of morality to psychopathy is that psychopaths appear to be deficient in only two components of morality, namely moral feelings and behavior; there is little doubt that they know, on a cognitive level, what society considers to be right and wrong. However, being deficient in the conditioning of emotional responses, they are unable to experience moral feelings with sufficient intensity for awareness of the rules of society to be reflected in behavior. Referring back to the Solomon et al. (1968) study, it is of some interest that dogs punished late in the response sequence learned *which food was taboo* just as rapidly as did those punished early in the sequence. However, for the late-punished dogs this knowledge did not result in much resistance to temptation (moral behavior).

> The authors assume that the dogs, even with long delays of punishment, quickly "know" which food results in punishment administered by the experimenter. This is a type of cognitive learning that can span long temporal intervals. The dogs *know* what they are not supposed to eat! However, when the experimenter is missing, and the dogs are faced with an uncertainty and change in the controlling stimulus situation, the authors' argument is that cognition is not enough. The hungry dogs cannot be certain any longer that eating the taboo horsemeat will result in punishment, because the experimenter is gone. It is under these conditions of changed social stimulation that the authors believe the conditioned emotional reactions of the dogs "take over" (Solomon et al., 1968, p. 237).

Presumably, these conditioned emotional reactions are too poorly developed in the psychopath to "take over" and to provide the motivation for good conduct when he is on his own.

Incidentally, we might describe the neurotic delinquent, within Brown's conception of morality, as one who has good knowledge of the rules, strong feelings, but poor conduct, a combination that could arise through (1) punishment relatively late in the response sequence, that is, at point *C* in Figure 19, and (2) a normal capacity to acquire conditioned emotional responses. Similarly, the socialized or dyssocial criminal could be described as an individual who has good knowledge of the rules of the subculture he lives in, strong moral feelings, and good conduct according to the standards of his own subculture. That is, he is abnormal only because he has learned a set of rules that is incompatible with the larger society in which he lives.

Modeling

Recent social learning theories (Aronfreed, 1968; Bandura and Walters, 1963) have placed a great deal of emphasis on the role of modeling in the development of social behavior. Both theory and research clearly indicate that observation of a model's behavior and its consequent rewards and punishments can result in the inhibition of responses in the observer's repertoire, the elicitation of previously inhibited responses, and the transmission of novel responses from model to observer.

Accordingly, we might assume that at least part of a psychopath's behavior results from modeling another individual's psychopathic behavior. The finding by Robins (1966) that the parents of psychopaths are often themselves antisocial or psychopathic is consistent with this suggestion.[2] Buss (1966) makes the point that two types of parental behavior are important to a modeling theory of psychopathy. One is a cold, distant relationship with the child; through modeling, the child learns only the formal superficial attributes of social situations (recall that Greenacre, 1945, suggested something similar). The other is inconsistency of the parents in providing affection, rewards, and punishments; the child does not have a consistent model to imitate and consequently his concept of "self" remains diffuse and inconsistent (see Gough's role-taking theory discussed earlier).

Delay of Gratification

The ability to delay gratification of needs and impulses is related to a variety of antecedent conditions and personality characteristics. Mischel (1966) has reviewed much of the relevant research and has outlined a theory of self-imposed delay of reward based on Rotter's (1954) social learning theory. Thus, whether an individual will delay gratification is assumed to depend on his expectancy that reward will be obtained and on the incentive value of the reward. As we might expect, the ability to delay gratification is positively related to ego-strength, resistance to temptation, and social responsibility.

---

[2] A simple modeling theory of psychopathy is weakened by the evidence (Robins, 1966) that paternal antisocial behavior is related to psychopathy in both the male and female offspring. It is not clear, in this case, why both sexes should model the behavior of the father.

According to Mischel, expectancies about delayed rewards in any given situation are based on the individual's experiences in similar situations and on observation or inference of the consequences to live or symbolic models for various patterns of behavior. In terms of the theory then, we might expect that the psychopath's well-known inability to delay gratification is related to generally low expectancy for rewards that are delayed. There are several ways in which a situation of this type could develop. The most obvious is that the child may simply model the behavior of parents whose behavior is geared to the immediate satisfaction of needs. That behavior of this sort often leads to future unfortunate consequences for the parent may not be at all obvious to the young child. The parents' behavior towards the child may also be important. For instance, if they continually give in to the child's demands, he may miss the opportunity of learning to work and wait for long-term rewards (Maher, 1966). Alternatively, the psychopath may have had rewards frequently promised but seldom delivered, resulting in a generalized low expectancy for delayed reward and a tendency therefore to "get it while you can." In other words, promised rewards are no rewards.

Arieti (1967) has hypothesized that a child learns to postpone gratification by being consistently trained to expect substitute gratifications at progressively increasing intervals. Instead of immediate reward, the child receives his mother's love and approval and a promise that something good will happen to him as a reward for not giving in immediately to his impulsive urges. As Arieti stated:

> Promises and hopes, although visualizations of things which have not materialized, retain a flavor or echo of mother's approval and tenderness.[3] Now it could be that . . . psychopaths did not go through these normal stages. What appeared to the child as deprivation held no compensations. The postponement was enforced in a crude way. No benevolent mother was there to help the child to make the transition from immediate gratification to postponement. He did not learn to expect approval and tenderness, to experience hope and to anticipate the fulfillment of a promise (pp. 305–306).

To summarize the preceding points, it is possible that the psychopath's inability to delay gratification is related to a family background in which impulse-control training was generally poor and in which parental models themselves displayed little delay capacity.

Several investigators have been concerned with establishing a relationship between the ability to delay gratification and the extent to which an individual is oriented toward future events. In one study (Klineberg, 1968)

---

[3] The learning theorist would say that the verbal stimuli (promises) have acquired secondary reward value through their association with the mother's love and attention.

the tendency to select a large, delayed reward instead of a smaller, immediate one was directly related to the degree of everyday preoccupation with future events, and the degree to which images of personal future events were endowed with a sense of reality. Concerning the latter point, the psychopath's limited fantasy resources would probably make it difficult for him to imagine future events with sufficient vividness for them to have a sense of reality. If the future is vague and unreal to the psychopath, the present is not, and he therefore concerns himself solely with what is real to him.

A final point is relevant here. Hare's (1965a) model of psychopathy outlined in Chapter 6 (Figure 15) also accounts for the psychopath's tendency to satisfy immediate needs, although this behavior was assumed to reflect classical conditioning mechanisms. The earlier analysis is not necessarily incompatible with the ones discussed in this chapter.

SUMMARY

Although many psychopaths come from broken, impoverished homes and have experienced some form of parental loss and rejection, it appears that one of the best predictors of adult psychopathy is having a father who was himself psychopathic, alcoholic, or antisocial.

Several theorists have suggested that the psychopath is pathologically unable to role-play and that his early experiences lead him to learn a social facade with no moral or emotional constraints other than what looks good to others.

The psychopath's apparent lack of guilt for transgressions and his low resistance to temptation are interpreted as the result of parental discipline and punishment that are considerably delayed and perhaps administered inconsistently.

It has also been suggested that the psychopath's inability to delay gratification may be related to a family background in which impulse-control training was generally poor and in which parental models themselves displayed little capacity to delay.

CHAPTER EIGHT

THE MODIFICATION
OF PSYCHOPATHIC BEHAVIOR

Although they may appear unduly pessimistic, the following comments are probably representative of the majority of clinical opinion and experience:

> Over a period of many years I have remained discouraged about the effect of treatment on the psychopath. Having regularly failed in my own efforts to help such patients alter their fundamental pattern of inadequacy and antisocial activity, I had hoped for a while that treatment by others would be more successful. I have had the opportunity to see patients who were treated by psychoanalysis, by psychoanalytically oriented psychotherapy, by group and by milieu therapy, and by other variations of dynamic method. I have seen some patients who were treated for years. I have also known cases in which not only the patient but various members of his family were given prolonged psychotherapy. None of these measures impressed me as achieving successful results. The psychopaths continued to behave as they had behaved in the past (Cleckley, 1964, pp. 476–477).

The results of most empirical studies are equally discouraging (see review by McCord and McCord, 1964). Thus, with few exceptions, the traditional forms of psychotherapy, including psychoanalysis, group therapy, client-centered therapy, psychodrama, have proved ineffective in the treatment of psychopathy. Nor have the biological therapies, including psychosurgery, electroshock therapy, and the use of various drugs, fared much better.

In many respects it is hardly surprising that psychotherapy is not effective in the modification of psychopathic behavior. The reasons for this statement are related to certain assumptions about the nature of the psychotherapeutic process. Although the various psychotherapies differ in many ways, they have several things in common that have been nicely summarized by Patterson (1966). These similarities are listed below, along with comments about their relevance to psychopathy.

1. The various therapies recognize that the patient's neurosis, maladjustment, disturbance, and so forth, are personally distressing and painful and that he consequently attempts to change it. Although personal distress may be involved in many forms of psychopathology, we have seen that it is seldom an important consideration in psychopathy. Moreover, the psychopath generally sees nothing wrong with his behavior and is therefore hardly likely to be motivated toward changing it.

2. It is recognized that the patient's present behavior is influenced by expectations about its future consequences. A considerable amount of evidence has already been presented to indicate that the psychopath is present-oriented and that his behavior is not guided by the possibility of future consequences.

3. It is recognized that psychotherapy involves a complex interpersonal relationship between therapist and patient, and that this relationship is *affective* as well as cognitive and intellectual in nature. The psychopath is apparently incapable of the empathy, warmth, and sincerity needed to develop the type of emotional relationship required for effective therapy. Nor is he likely to actively participate in, or become deeply and personally involved in, the therapeutic process.

4. It is also recognized that both therapist and patient expect therapy to produce beneficial results. With respect to psychopathy, doubts and scepticism about its treatability are widespread, and it is possible that this negative attitude, when present, decreases the chances that therapy will be effective.

There are several other reasons why therapy is ineffective with psychopathic individuals. We have already noted that such individuals see nothing wrong with their behavior, and that they often find their behavior extremely rewarding, at least in the short run—being caught and punished periodically, usually well after the act, does little to offset the immediate reinforcement obtained. Moreover, the hedonistic and self-centered acts of many psychopaths often go relatively unpunished. Studies by Robins (1966) and Gibbens, Briscoe, and Dell (1968) have shown that a surprisingly large number of psychopathic persons somehow manage to avoid incarceration in spite of the fact that their behavior may be grossly antisocial. In many cases they are protected by family and friends who may themselves be their victims. In other cases they may be charming and intelligent enough to talk their way out of prosecution. In any event, their behavior may be relatively unchecked and unpunished; and therefore very rewarding, persistent, and firmly established.

All of these considerations suggest that psychopaths are extremely poor candidates for psychotherapy. However, it is possible that therapy with these individuals could be made more effective by convincing them that their behavior is self-defeating, increasing their appreciation of the future consequences of present action, and exerting complete control over the administration of rewards and punishments. Such an approach, while feasible, is of course more attractive on a theoretical than on a practical level. Consider, for example, the method suggested by Thorne (1959). On the assumption that the psychopath's behavior reflects a maladaptive *life style* that is maintained by reinforcement from family, friends, and associates, Thorne has outlined what he considers to be the requirements of successful therapy with psychopaths. These are summarized as follows.

1. The therapist must have complete control over the financial resources of the psychopath, usually by being made trustee of his accounts.

2. Relatives and other interested parties must agree not to bail the psychopath out of his difficulties; he must be required to face the consequences of his own behavior.

3. The therapist must be very persistent in gradually getting the psychopath to exert some limits and controls over his own behavior.

4. The therapist should not protect the psychopath from the legal and social consequences of his actions.

5. The therapist should make it clear to the psychopath that he understands him thoroughly, knows what to expect, and will be convinced of his good intentions only through actions and not words.

6. The psychopath must be shown repeatedly that his behavior is self-defeating.

7. The therapist should search for a leverage point to stimulate more socially acceptable behavior. As a last resort, the therapist may have to use money, which he controls, as an incentive.

In addition to these points, Thorne suggested that a great deal of patience, time, and money are required; in several cases, an investment of $15,000 per year for as long as 10 years was needed to effect a satisfactory outcome. It is not surprising therefore that no controlled research using Thorne's methods has been carried out; the investment in time and money is far too great and, many would say, not worth the effort.

THERAPEUTIC COMMUNITIES

Since most of the psychopath's problems involve conflicts with society instead of any personal distress, we might expect that the traditional forms of individual psychotherapy would be less effective than treatment designed to improve interpersonal relations. To a certain extent this latter, broader type of treatment is what is involved in the program outlined by Thorne. Other programs have attempted to improve the psychopath's social behavior by placing him in some sort of *therapeutic community* or by using *milieu therapy,* the rationale being that socialization of the psychopath requires a complete restructing of his social and psychological environment.

McCord and McCord (1964) describe milieu therapy, as used with child psychopaths at New York's Wiltwyck School, as follows.

> Milieu therapy mobilizes the entire environment against the child's disorder. Psychotherapy, group therapy, and art therapy, social workers, counselors, and psychologists converge in treating the child. Moreover, the treatment necessarily removes the child from his family and his social environment. Consequently, one finds it difficult to isolate particular causes of change. Yet, one can suggest that four factors may play primary roles in altering the boys: the rapport between children and counselors; the absence of punitive frustration; the subtle but powerful social control exerted not only by the adults but also by the boys' leaders; and individual and group psychotherapy (1964, p. 161).

On the basis of a study of 15 psychopathic children treated at Wiltwyck, the McCords concluded that milieu therapy could be reasonably effective. Briefly, there was a decrease in aggressive fantasies and behavior, an increase in internalized guilt and control over impulsivity, and an improvement in ego ideals and in attitudes toward authority. Unfortunately, however, no adequate control group was available for comparison.

A study by Craft, Stephenson, and Granger (1964) compared the effectiveness of two different forms of residential treatment at Balderton Hospital, England. Fifty psychopathic males, aged 13 to 25, were alternately assigned to one of two treatment regimes.[1] One regime was essentially self-governing and included intensive group psychotherapy and tolerant staff members. The other regime was more authoritarian and included

---

[1] Most of the subjects were of below average intelligence, as measured by the Wechsler test. Although many of these subjects may not have been psychopaths (as the term is used in this book), the Craft et al. study is presented because of the thoroughness with which it was carried out and because of its implications for treating psychopathy.

a firm but sympathetic form of discipline and only superficial individual psychotherapy. After about six to nine months of treatment, patients in each regime were permitted to obtain day jobs in the community, returning each night to the hospital. Discharge occurred after about one year of treatment. Psychological testing indicated that neither group showed appreciable personality or adjustment changes during the treatment program. However, a follow-up study made one year after discharge found that those treated under the authoritarian regime had been convicted of significantly fewer offenses after release than had those in the self-governing regime. Craft et al. concluded that work training in a friendly but disciplined residential setting is probably more effective in the treatment of psychopathy than is work training combined with group psychotherapy in a permissive setting.

Several institutions have reported good results using authoritarian regimes. Perhaps the best known is Herstedvester, a Danish maximum-security institution for the treatment of chronic criminals, including those who are psychopathic. As described by its superintendent, the treatment at Herstedvester includes stern discipline, individual and group psychotherapy, and intensive training in appropriate social behavior and interpersonal relationships (Sturup, 1964). Since sentences at the institution are indeterminate, averaging about two and one-half years, therapy is both intensive and extensive; moreover, it is followed up by well-developed after-care services designed to help integrate the inmates into the community. Under these conditions, about 50 percent of any given group of discharged inmates manage to function satisfactorily in society. Moreover, of 900 chronic criminals incarcerated between 1935 and 1953, less than 10 percent still remained in detention in 1963. How many of the remainder had died or had left the country is not known.

Other institutions have also attempted to socialize chronic and disturbed criminals. For example, a Dutch therapeutic community near Utrecht provides "mentally disturbed" criminals, including psychopaths, with intensive individual, group, and community therapy (Arendsen Hein, 1959). Patients are given a great deal of freedom but are held responsible for the way in which they use it, and are subjected to intense group pressures toward conforming to the wishes and needs of the community as a whole. For this reason, the institution has been called a "sociotherapeutic" or "resocialization" community. Similar to the procedure at Herstedvester, discharge is followed by intensive after-care. Arendsen Hein (1959) reports that about 38 percent of the "criminal psychopaths" improve enough to be sent back into society, and that the remission rate one year after discharge is very low.

The apparent success experienced by these therapeutic communities is encouraging, although optimism should be tempered by the fact that many of the patients involved were probably not psychopaths in the same sense that the term has been used throughout this book.

SPONTANEOUS IMPROVEMENT

There is another reason for being cautious about accepting at face value the results obtained by the therapeutic communities. It is well known that the recovery rate of neurotics who have received psychotherapy is no better than that of similar patients who have received no treatment at all (Eysenck, 1961). In each case about two-thirds of the patients show some degree of improvement.

In view of the generally negative results obtained with psychopaths, it may be thought that comparisons with spontaneous improvement rates are not needed. However, there is some evidence that the persistence and immutability of psychopathic behavior may be somewhat overemphasized, and that the negative results obtained in many studies reflect a sampling bias. Robins (1966) found that only a small proportion of the psychopathic population is actually referred to psychiatrists, and that those who are referred have a worse prognosis than those who are not. The reason for the difference in prognosis is that a psychopath is likely to see a psychiatrist only when he is in trouble and referred by the courts or some other agency. It is possible that those who are so referred represent the worst elements of the psychopathic population—at least their behavior is of the sort that requires public intervention. Moreover, few psychopaths remain in treatment very long; as soon as the legal crisis is resolved, they generally terminate treatment. The magnitude of this treatment bias can be quite appreciable. Among the psychopaths studied by Robins (1966), 57 percent of those who had received no psychiatric treatment showed some signs of improvement in behavior, whereas only 22 percent of those who had received treatment improved.

Other data reported by Robins are of interest. About a third of the psychopaths studied showed a reduction in the range and severity of antisocial behavior as they aged, with improvement occurring most often between the ages of 30 and 40. Although they were less trouble to the police and the various social agencies, many of those who showed improvement still remained relatively difficult and disagreeable individuals. In discussing the variables related to improvement, Robins commented that many of the subjects attributed the change to

. . . fear of further punishment or to loyalty to their spouses. Statistical association supported their explanation that marriage and brief sentences seemed

related to improvement. While the current study offers no airtight demonstra-
tion for the powers of social control and fear of punishment as effective
correctives to antisocial behavior, the positive relations found between social
participation with spouse, sibling, friends, and neighbors and improvement
makes it appear at least hopeful that supporting the pressures towards con-
formity in the sociopath's social environment and trying to prevent his becoming isolated from family, friends, and neighbors may be helpful in limit-
ing his antisocial activities. Such goals at least appear more consistent with
the current findings than do the goals of increased hospitalization or more
psychotherapy, neither of which showed any positive association with improvement. If hospitalization and current psychotherapeutic techniques are
not helpful, manipulation of the social environment may provide one hopeful
alternative to patiently awaiting the "burning out" of antisocial interests,
which frequently comes so late in life, if it comes at all, that enormous damage has been done both to the life of the patient and the lives of those with
whom he interacts (Robins, 1966, p. 236).

In many respects, of course, the manipulation of the social environment suggested by Robins is the rationale used by the therapeutic communities already discussed. It is possible, therefore, that at least part of
their results reflect the increased social control these communities exert
over their patients. An additional possibility is that much of the apparent
therapeutic effect of these institutions represents the "burning out" of antisocial activity that sometimes occurs with age.[2] Note, for example, that the
improvement rates obtained at Herstedvester and Utrecht are not that
much greater than those found by Robins, particularly when it is recognized that these institutions probably handle a large proportion of nonpsychopathic inmates whose recovery rate may be greater than that of psychopaths.

BEHAVIOR THERAPY

Many of those who have become disenchanted with the traditional forms
of psychotherapy have been encouraged by the often dramatic claims of
the behavior therapists. Behavior therapy involves the use of conditioning
principles and procedures to modify pathological behavior (see Bandura,
1961; Eysenck and Rachman, 1965), and seems particularly effective in
the treatment of neurotic symptoms, including excessive anxiety, phobias,
tics, and sexual deviation.

Thus far, few attempts have been made to use behavior therapy tech-

---

[2] Besides the influence of social control, it is possible that the improvement some psychopaths show with age results from the delayed but coincident attainment of cortical
and social maturation (see Chapter 3).

niques with psychopathy, perhaps because very little of the psychopath's behavior is as specific as the symptoms found in the neuroses. In one study, however, an attempt was made to modify the homosexual behavior of 32 patients, including seven who appear to have been psychopathic, by using aversive or avoidance conditioning (MacCulloch and Feldman, 1966). Pictures of males were flashed on a screen and were followed eight seconds later by an electric shock. However, shock could be avoided by pressing a lever that removed the picture of the male and replaced it with a picture of a female. The details of the conditioning procedure, including the intensity of shock, number of trials, and so forth, were not given. Nevertheless, on the basis of verbalized attitudes and behavioral adjustment, the authors reported that more than half of the subjects derived some benefit from the treatment. However, no improvement was shown by the psychopathic subjects. This is not an unexpected finding, since the aversive conditioning paradigm used involves the classical conditioning of fear and the reinforcement of avoidance responses by fear reduction. As noted in Chapter 4, psychopaths perform poorly in such situations.

MacCulloch and Feldman suggested that the performance of psychopathic subjects might be improved with the use of a stimulant such as amphetamine. This is a plausible suggestion, at least in the short run, since Schachter and Latané (1964), in a study discussed in Chapter 4, found that adrenalin considerably improved the performance of psychopathic criminals on an avoidance learning task. Although behavior therapy is generally used to reduce anxiety or to remove symptoms, it could conceivably be used to do just the opposite with psychopaths. If we assume that the antisocial behavior of these individuals results partly from a failure to acquire conditioned fear responses in certain social situations, therapy could take the form of increasing fear and anxiety, possibly with the assistance of drugs such as adrenalin and amphetamine. The simultaneous use of operant conditioning techniques to assist in the development of prosocial forms of behavior might also prove fruitful. Schwitzgebel (1967) has shown, for example, that social reinforcement can be used to advantage in the modification of delinquent behavior. Although psychopaths are probably less influenced by social reinforcements than are most individuals, techniques such as those used by Peters and Jenkins (1954) might be beneficial. In this study chronic schizophrenics were given subshock injections of insulin and then rewarded with candy for good performance on a series of tasks, including those associated with the solution of interpersonal problems. The use of this procedure resulted in an increase in the effectiveness of social rewards and an improvement in social relationships. Whether similar results would be obtained with psychopaths is an empirical question. However, it might be worthwhile to set up an intensive, long-term treatment program, patterned after the therapeutic communities found in Denmark and Holland, but including attempts to increase the motivating influence of fear and anxiety and to make social reinforcements more effective.

SUMMARY

The traditional therapeutic procedures have not been effective in changing the behavior of psychopaths. A possible exception to this generally pessimistic outcome is the use of some sort of "therapeutic community" in which an attempt is made to improve the psychopath's interpersonal relations and to restructure his social environment. Evidence also exists that the apparent persistence and immutability of the psychopath's behavior may be somewhat overemphasized, and that, in some cases, a gradual reduction in the severity of antisocial behavior occurs with age.

REFERENCES

Albert, R.S., Brigante, T.R., & Chase, M. The psychopathic personality: A content analysis of the concept. *Journal of General Psychology,* 1959, **60,** 17–28.

American Psychiatric Association. *Diagnostic and statistical manual: Mental disorders.* Washington, D.C.: APA, 1952.

Andry, R.G. Faulty paternal- and maternal-child relationships, affection and delinquency. *British Journal of Delinquency,* 1957, **8,** 34–48.

Andry, R.G. *Delinquency and parental pathology.* London: Methuen, 1960.

Arendsen Hein, G. Group therapy with criminal psychopaths. *Acta Psychotherapeutica,* Supplement, 1959, **7,** 6–16.

Arieti, S. *The intrapsychic self.* New York: Basic Books, 1967.

Aronfreed, J. *Conduct and conscience.* New York: Academic Press, 1968.

Arthurs, R.G.S., & Cahoon, E.B. A clinical and electroencephalographic survey of psychopathic personality. *American Journal of Psychiatry,* 1964, **120,** 875–882.

Ax, A.F. Psychophysiological methodology for the study of schizophrenia. In R. Ressler & N. Greenfield (Eds.), *Physiological correlates of psychological disorder.* Madison: University of Wisconsin Press, 1962. Pp. 29–44.

Bandura, A. Psychotherapy as a learning process. *Psychological Bulletin,* 1961, **58,** 143–149.

Bandura, A., & Walters, R.H. *Social learning and personality development.* New York: Holt, Rinehart & Winston, Inc., 1963.

Barnes, C.D. The interaction of amphetamine and eserine on the EEG. *Life Sciences,* 1966, **5,** 1897–1902.

Bay-Rakal, S. The significance of EEG abnormality in behavior problem children. *Canadian Psychiatric Association Journal,* 1965, **10,** 387–391.

Bell, R. A reinterpretation of the direction of effects in studies of socialization. *Psychological Review,* 1968, **75,** 81–95.

Bennet, I. *Delinquent and neurotic children.* London: Tavistock Publications, 1960.

119

Berg, P.S. Neurotic and psychopathic criminals: Some measures of ego syntonicity, impulse socialization and perceptual consistency. Unpublished doctoral dissertation. Michigan State University, 1963.

Berlyne, D. Curiosity and exploration. *Science,* 1966, **153,** 25–33.

Bernard, J.L., & Eisenman, R. Verbal conditioning in sociopaths with social and monetary reinforcement. *Journal of Personality and Social Psychology,* 1967, **6,** 203–206.

Blaylock, J.J. Verbal conditioning performance of psychopaths and nonpsychopaths under verbal reward and punishment. Unpublished doctoral dissertation. State University of Iowa, 1960.

Block, J. A study of affective-responsiveness in a lie detection situation. *Journal of Abnormal and Social Psychology,* 1957, **55,** 11–15.

Block, J.D. Monozygotic twin similarity in multiple psychophysiologic parameters and measures. In J. Wortis (Ed.), *Recent advances in biological psychiatry.* Vol. 9. New York: Plenum Press, 1967. Pp. 105–118.

Blackburn, R. Personality in relation to extreme aggression in psychiatric offenders. *British Journal of Psychiatry,* 1968, **114,** 821–828.

Broverman, D., Klaiber, E., Kobayaski, Y., & Vogel, W. Roles of activation and inhibition in sex differences in cognitive abilities. *Psychological Review,* 1968, **75,** 23–50.

Brown, R. *Social psychology.* New York: Free Press, 1965.

Brown, J.S., & Farber, I.E. Secondary motivational systems. In P.R. Farnsworth (Ed.), *Annual review of psychology.* Vol. 19. Palo Alto: Annual Reviews, Inc., 1968. Pp. 99–134.

Bryan, J.H., & Kapche, R. Psychopathy and verbal conditioning. *Journal of Abnormal Psychology,* 1967, **72,** 71–73.

Buss, A.H. *Psychopathology.* New York: Wiley, 1966.

Cleckley, H. *The mask of sanity* (4th ed.). St. Louis, Mo.: Mosby, 1964.

Cook, J.O., & Barnes, L.W. Choice of delay of inevitable shock. *Journal of Abnormal and Social Psychology,* 1964, **68,** 669–672.

Craddick, R.A. Wechsler-Bellevue I.Q. scores of psychopathic and non-psychopathic prisoners. *Journal of Psychological Studies,* 1961, **12,** 167–172.

Craddick, R. Selection of psychopathic from non-psychopathic prisoners within a Canadian prison. *Psychological Reports,* 1962, **10,** 495–499.

Craft, M.J. *Ten studies into psychopathic personality.* Bristol: John Wright, 1965.

Craft, M., Stephenson, G., & Granger, C. A controlled trial of authoritarian and self-governing regimes with adolescent psychopaths. *American Journal of Orthopsychiatry,* 1964, **34,** 543–554.

Dahlstrom, W.M., & Welch, G.S. *An MMPI handbook: A guide to use in clinical practice and research.* University of Minnesota Press, Minneapolis, 1960.

Douglas, R.J. The hippocampus and behavior. *Psychological Bulletin,* 1967, **67,** 416–442.

Edelberg, R. The relationship between the galvanic skin response, vaso-constriction, and tactile sensitivity. *Journal of Experimental Psychology,* 1961, **62,** 187–195.

Ehrlich, S.K., & Keogh, R.P. The psychopath in a mental institution. *Archives of Neurology and Psychiatry,* 1956, **76,** 286–295.

Ellingson, R.J. Incidence of EEG abnormality among patients with mental disorders of apparently nonorganic origin: A criminal review. *American Journal of Psychiatry,* 1954, **111,** 263–275.

Ephron, H., and Carrington, P., Rapid eye movement sleep and cortical homeostasis. *Psychological Review,* 1966, **73,** 500–526.

Eysenck, H.J. *The Maudsley Personality Inventory.* London: University of London Press, 1959.

Eysenck, H.J. (Ed.). *Handbook of abnormal psychology.* New York: Basic Books, 1961.

Eysenck, H.J. The effects of psychotherapy. In H.J. Eysenck (Ed.), *Handbook of abnormal psychology.* New York: Basic Books, 1961. Pp. 697–725.

Eysenck, H.J. *Crime and personality.* London: Methuen, 1964.

Eysenck, H.J. *The biological basis of personality.* Springfield, Ill.: Charles C. Thomas, 1967.

Eysenck, H.J., & Rachman, S. *The causes and cures of neurosis.* London: Routledge & Kegan Paul, 1965.

Fairweather, G.W. The effect of selected incentive conditions on the performance of psychopathic, neurotic, and normal criminals in a serial rote learning situation. Unpublished doctoral dissertation. University of Illinois, 1953.

Fine, B.J., & Sweeney, D.R. Personality traits, and situational factors, and catecholamine excretion. *Journal of Experimental Research in Personality,* 1968, **3,** 15–27.

Finney, J.C. Relations and meaning of the new MMPI scales. *Psychological Reports,* 1966, **18,** 459–470.

Fisher, G.M. Discrepancy in verbal-performance I.Q. in adolescent psychopaths. *Journal of Clinical Psychology,* 1961, **17,** 60–61.

Fisher, S. Projective methodologies. In P.R. Farnsworth (Ed.), *Annual Review of Psychology.* Vol. 18. Palo Alto: Annual Reviews, Inc., 1967. Pp. 165–190.

Fiske, D.W., & Maddi, S.R. *Functions of varied experience.* Homewood, Ill.: Dorsey, 1961.

Forssman, H., and Frey, T.S. Electroencephalograms of boys with behavior disorders. *Acta Psychiat. Neurol. Scand.,* 1953, **28,** 61–73.

Foulds, G.A. *Personality and personal illness.* London: Tavistock Publications, 1965.

Fox, R., & Lippert, W. Spontaneous GSR and anxiety level in sociopathic delinquents. *Journal of Consulting Psychology,* 1963, **27,** 368.

Freud, S. *The problem of anxiety.* New York: Norton, 1936.

Gellhorn, E. *Autonomic imbalance and the hypothalamus: Implications for physiology, medicine, psychology, and neuropsychiatry.* Minneapolis: University of Minnesota Press, 1957.

Gibbens, T.C.N., Briscoe, O., & Dell, S. Psychopathic and neurotic offenders in mental hospitals. In A.V.S. de Reuck & R. Porter (Eds.), *The mentally abnormal offender.* London: J. & A. Churchill, 1968. Pp. 143–149.

Gibbens, T.C.N., Pond, D.A., & Stafford-Clark, D. A follow-up study of criminal psychopaths. *British Journal of Delinquency,* 1955, **5,** 126–136.

Goldstein, I.B. The relationship of muscle tension and autonomic activity to psychiatric disorders. *Psychosomatic Medicine,* 1965, **27,** 39–52.

Gottesman, I. Genetic variation in adaptive personality traits. *Journal of Child Psychology and Psychiatry,* 1966, **7,** 199–208.

Gough, H.G. A sociological theory of psychopathy. *American Journal of Sociology,* 1948, **53,** 359–366.

Gough, H.G. *Manual for the California Psychological Inventory.* Palo Alto: Consulting Psychologists Press, 1957.

Gough, H.G. Theory and measurement of socialization. *Journal of Consulting Psychology,* 1960, **24,** 23–30.

Grant, D.A. Classical and operant conditioning. In A.W. Melton (Ed.), *Categories of human learning.* New York: Academic Press, 1964. Pp. 3–31.

Grant, D.A. Adding communication to the signalling property of the CS in classical conditioning. Paper read at American Psychological Association Meeting, Washington, D.C., September, 1967.

Gray, K.C., & Hutchison, H.C. The psychopathic personality: A survey of Canadian psychiatrists' opinions. *Canadian Psychiatric Association Journal,* 1964, **9,** 452–461.

Greenacre, P. Conscience in the psychopath. *American Journal of Orthopsychiatry,* 1945, **15,** 495–509.

Greer, S. Study of parental loss in neurotics and sociopaths. *Archives of General Psychiatry,* 1964, **11,** 177–180.

Gregory, I. Studies of parental deprivation in psychiatric patients. *American Journal of Psychiatry,* 1958, **115,** 432–442.

Grossman, S.B. *A textbook of physiological psychology.* New York: Wiley, 1967.

Group for the Advancement of Psychiatry. *Psychopathological disorders in children: Theoretical considerations and a proposed classification.* New York: Author, 1966. Report No. 62.

Guilford, J.P. Intelligence: 1965 model. *American Psychologist,* 1966, **21,** 20–26.

Gurvitz, M. Wechsler-Bellevue test and the diagnosis of psychopathic personality. *Journal of Clinical Psychology,* 1950, **6,** 397–401.

Hare, R.D. A conflict and learning theory analysis of psychopathic behavior. *Journal of Research in Crime and Delinquency,* 1965, **2,** 12–19 (a).

Hare, R.D. Acquisition and generalization of a conditioned-fear response in psychopathic and non-psychopathic criminals. *Journal of Psychology,* 1965, **59,** 367–370 (b).

Hare, R.D. Temporal gradient of fear arousal in psychopaths. *Journal of Abnormal Psychology,* 1965, **70,** 442–445 (c).

Hare, R.D. Psychopathy, fear arousal and anticipated pain. *Psychological Reports,* 1965, **16,** 499–502 (d).

Hare, R.D. Psychopathy and choice of immediate versus delayed punishment. *Journal of Abnormal Psychology,* 1966, **71,** 25–29 (a).

Hare, R.D. Preference for delay of shock as a function of its intensity and probability. *Psychonomic Science,* 1966, **5,** 393–394 (b).

Hare, R.D. Psychopathy, autonomic functioning, and the orienting response. *Journal of Abnormal Psychology* Monograph Supplement, 1968, **73,** No. 3, Part 2, 1–24 (a).

Hare, R.D. Detection threshold for electric shock in psychopaths. *Journal of Abnormal Psychology,* 1968, **73,** 268–272 (b).

Hare, R.D. An MMPI comparison of psychopathic and nonpsychopathic criminals. Unpublished data, 1969.

Hare, R.D., & Hare, Averil, S. Psychopathic behavior: A bibliography. *Excerpta Criminologica,* 1967, **7,** 365–386.

Hare, R.D., & Petrusic, W.M. Subjective intensity of electric shock as a function of delay in administration. Paper read at Western Psychological Association Meeting, San Francisco, May, 1967.

Hare, R.D., & Thorvaldson, S.A. Psychopathy and sensitivity to electrical stimulation. *Journal of Abnormal Psychology,* in press.

Harter, M.R. Excitability cycles and cortical scanning: A review of two hypotheses of central intermittency in perception. *Psychological Bulletin,* 1967, **68,** 47–58.

Hetherington, E.M., & Klinger, E. Psychopathy and punishment. *Journal of Abnormal and Social Psychology,* 1964, **69,** 113–115.

Hill, D. Ampetamine in psychopathic states. *British Journal of Addiction,* 1947, **44,** 50–54.

Hill, D. EEG in episodic psychotic and psychopathic behavior: A classification of data. *EEG and Clinical Neurophysiology,* 1952, **4,** 419–442.

Hill, D., & Watterson, D. Electroencephalographic studies of the psychopathic personality. *Journal of Neurology and Psychiatry,* 1942, **5,** 47–64.

Holzberg, J., & Hahn, F. The Picture-Frustration Technique as a measure of hostility and guilt reactions in adolescent psychopaths. *American Journal of Orthopsychiatry,* 1952, **22,** 776–795.

Hughes, J.R. A review of the positive spike phenomenon. In W. Wilson (Ed.), *Applications of electroencephalography in psychiatry.* Durham, N.C.: Duke University Press, 1965. Pp. 54–101.

Ingham, J., & Robinson, J. Personality in the diagnosis of hysteria. *British Journal of Psychology,* 1964, **55,** 276–284.

Irwin, S. A rational framework for the development, evaluation, and use of psychoactive drugs. *American Journal of Psychiatry,* 1968, **124** (Supplement on Drug Therapy), pp. 1–19.

Jenkins, R.L. Diagnosis, dynamics, and treatment in child psychiatry. *Psychiatric Research Reports,* 1964, **18,** 91–120.

Jenkins, R.L. Psychiatric syndromes in children and their relation to family background. *American Journal of Orthopsychiatry,* 1966, **36,** 450–457.

Johns, J.H., & Quay, H.C. The effect of social reward on verbal conditioning in psychopathic and neurotic military offenders. *Journal of Consulting Psychology,* 1962, **26,** 217–220.

Jung, J. *Verbal learning.* New York: Holt, Rinehart & Winston, 1968.

Kadlub, K.J. The effects of two types of reinforcements on the performance of psychopathic and normal criminals. Unpublished doctoral dissertation. University of Illinois, 1956.

Kagan, J. Personality development. In P. London and D. Rosenhan (eds.), *Foundations of abnormal psychology*. New York: Holt, Rinehart & Winston, 1968. Pp. 117–173.

Kanfer, F.H. Verbal conditioning. A review of its current status. In T. Dixon & D. Horton (Eds.), *Verbal behavior and general behavior theory*. New Jersey: Prentice-Hall, 1968. Pp. 245–290.

Kaplan, S.D. A visual analog of the Funkenstein test. *Archives of General Psychiatry*, 1960, **3**, 383–388.

Karpman, B. The structure of neurosis: with special differentials between neurosis, psychosis, homosexuality, alcoholism, psychopathy, and criminality. *Archives of Criminal Psychodynamics*, 1961, **4**, 599–646.

Kiloh, L. & Osselton, J.W. *Clinical electroencephalography*. Washington: Butterworth, 1966.

Kimble, G. *Hilgard and Marquis' conditioning and learning*. New York: Appleton-Century-Crofts, 1961.

Kimble, G. Categories of learning and the problem of definition. In A.W. Melton (Ed.), *Categories of human learning*. New York: Academic Press, 1964. Pp. 34–45.

Kimmel, H.D. Inhibition of the unconditioned response in classical conditioning. *Psychological Review*, 1966, **73**, 232–240.

Kimmel, H.D. Instrumental conditioning of autonomically mediated behavior. *Psychological Bulletin*, 1967, **67**, 337–345.

King, G. Differential autonomic responsiveness in the process-reactive classification of schizophrenia. *Journal of Abnormal and Social Psychology*, 1958, **56**, 160–164.

Kingsley, L. A comparative study of certain personality characteristics of psychopathic and non-psychopathic offenders. Unpublished doctoral dissertation. New York University, 1956.

Kingsley, L. A comparison of the sentence completion responses of psychopaths and prisoners. *Journal of Clinical Psychology*, 1961, **17**, 183–185.

Klein, G., Barr, H., & Wolitzky, D. Personality. In P.R. Farnsworth (Ed.). *Annual Review of Psychology*. Vol. 18. Palo Alto: Annual Reviews, Inc., 1967. Pp. 467–560.

Klineberg, S.L. Future time perspective and the preference for delayed reward. *Journal of Personality and Social Psychology*, 1968, **8**, 253–257.

Knott, J.R., Platt, E.B., Ashby, M.C., & Gottlieb, J.S. A familial evaluation of the electroencephalogram of patients with primary behavior disorder and psychopathic personality. *EEG and Clinical Neurophysiology*, 1953, **5**, 363–370.

Kurland, H.D., Yeager, C.T., & Arthur, R.J. Psychophysiologic aspects of severe behavior disorders. *Archives of General Psychiatry*, 1963, **8**, 599–604.

Lacey, J.I. Somatic response patterning and stress: Some revisions of activation theory. In M.H. Appley & R. Trumbull (Eds.), *Psychological stress: issues in research*. New York: Appleton-Century-Crofts, 1967. Pp. 14–44.

Lacey, J.I., & Lacey, B.C. The relationship of resting autonomic activity to motor impulsivity. In *The brain and human behavior* (proceedings of the Association for Research in Neural and Mental Disease). Baltimore: Williams & Wilkins, 1958. Pp. 144–209.

Lindner, R. Experimental studies in constitutional psychopathic inferiority. Part 1. Systemic patterns. *Journal of Criminal Psychopathology,* 1942, **3,** 252–276.

Lindsley, D.B. Psychological phenomena and the electroencephalogram. *EEG and Clinical Neurophysiology,* 1952, **4,** 443–456.

Lindsley, D.B. The ontogeny of pleasure: Neural and behavioral development. In R.G. Heath (Ed.), *The role of pleasure in behavior.* New York: Harper & Row, 1964. Pp. 3–22.

Lippert, W.W., & Senter, R.J. Electrodermal responses in the sociopath. *Psychonomic Science,* 1966, **4,** 25–26.

Lonstein, M.J. A Comparative study of level of aspiration variables in neurotic, psychopathic and normal subjects. Unpublished doctoral dissertation. University of Kentucky, 1952.

Lykken, D.T. *A study of anxiety in the sociopathic personality.* (Doctoral dissertation, University of Minnesota) Ann Arbor, Mich.: University Microfilms, 1955, No. 55–944.

Lykken, D.T. Neuropsychology and psychophysiology in personality research. In E.F. Borgatta & W.W. Lambert (Eds.), *Handbook of personality theory and research.* New York: Rand McNally, 1968.

Lynn, R. *Attention, arousal, and the orientation reaction.* London: Pergamon Press, 1966.

MacCulloch, M.J., & Feldman, M.P. Personality structure and its relation to success in the treatment of homosexuals by anticipatory avoidance conditioning. Unpublished manuscript. Crumpsall Hospital, Manchester, England, 1966.

MacKay, R.P. The temporal lobe and behavior. *Transactions and studies of the College of Physicians of Philadelphia,* 1965, **32,** 89–103.

McCleary, R.A. Response-modulating functions of the limbic system: initiation and suppression. In E. Stellar & J. Sprague (Eds.), *Progress in physiological psychology.* Vol. 1. New York: Academic Press, 1966. Pp. 209–272.

McCord, W., & McCord, J. *The psychopath: An essay on the criminal mind.* Princeton, N.J.: Van Nostrand, 1964.

McDonald, D.C., Johnson, L.C., & Hord, D.J. Habituation of the orienting response in alert and drowsy subjects. *Psychophysiology,* 1964, **1,** 163–173.

Maas, J.P. Cathexes towards significant others by sociopathic woman. *Archives of General Psychiatry,* 1966, **15,** 516–522.

Maher, B.A. *Principles of psychopathology.* New York: McGraw-Hill, 1966.

Malmo, R.B. Activation: A neuropsychological dimension. *Psychological Review,* 1959, **66,** 367–386.

Malmo, R.B. Studies of anxiety: Some clinical origins of the activation concept. In C.D. Spielberger (Ed.), *Anxiety and behavior.* New York: Academic Press, 1966. Pp. 157–178.

Manne, S.H., Kandel, A., & Rosenthal, D. Differences between performance I.Q. and verbal I.Q. in a severely sociopathic population. *Journal of Clinical Psychology,* 1962, **18,** 73–77.

Marcus, B. A dimensional study of a prison population. *British Journal of Criminology,* 1960, **1,** 130–153.

Marks, I. *Patterns of meaning in psychiatric patients: Semantic differential responses in obsessives and psychopaths.* Maudsley Monograph No. 13. London: University of Oxford Press, 1966.

Martin, I. Eyelid conditioning and concomitant GSR activity. *Behavior Research and Therapy,* 1963, **1,** 255–265.

Maughs, S.B. Concept of psychopathy and psychopathic personality: its evolution and historical development. *Journal of Criminal Psychopathology,* 1941, **2,** 329–356 and 465–399.

Melton, A.W. (Ed.) *Categories of human learning.* New York: Academic Press, 1964.

Melzack, R., & Wall, P.D. Pain mechanisms: A new theory. *Science,* 1965, **150,** 971–979.

Milgram, S. A behavioral study of obedience. *Journal of Abnormal and Social Psychology,* 1963, **67,** 371–378.

Miller, J.G. *Eyeblink conditioning of primary and neurotic psychopaths.* (Doctoral dissertation, University of Missouri) Ann Arbor, Mich.: University Microfilms, 1966. No. 67–923.

Miller, N.E. Experiments relevant to learning theory and psychopathology. Proceedings of the 18th International Congress of Psychology, Moscow, 1966.

Miller, N.E. Liberalization of basic S-R concepts: Extensions to conflict behavior, motivation and social learning. In S. Koch (Ed.), *Psychology: A study of a science.* Vol. 2. New York: McGraw-Hill, 1959.

Mischel, W. Theory and research on the antecedants of self-imposed delay of reward. In B.A. Maher (Ed.), *Progress in experimental personality research.* Vol. 3. New York: Academic Press, 1966. Pp. 85–130.

Montagu, A. Chromosomes and crime. *Psychology Today,* 1968, **2,** 42–49.

Morrison, D.F. *Multivariate statistical methods.* New York: McGraw-Hill, 1967.

Mowrer, O.H. On the dual nature of learning—a reinterpretation of "conditioning" and "problem-solving". *Harvard Educational Review,* 1947, **17,** 102–148.

Mowrer, O.H. *Learning theory and the symbolic processes.* New York: Wiley, 1960.

Oltman, J., & Friedman, S. Parental deprivation in psychiatric conditions, 111. *Diseases of the Nervous System,* 1967, **28,** 298–303.

Orris, J.B. Visual monitoring performance in three subgroups of male delinquents. Unpublished Master's thesis. University of Illinois, 1967.

Osgood, C.E., Suci, G.J. & Tannenbaum, P.H. *The measurement of meaning.* Urbana, Ill.: University of Illinois Press, 1957.

Painting, D.H. The performance of psychopathic individuals under conditions of positive and negative partial reinforcement. *Journal of Abnormal and Social Psychology,* 1961, **62,** 352–355.

Patterson, C.H. *Theories of counseling and psychotherapy.* New York: Harper & Row, 1966.

Pennington, L.A. Psychopathic and criminal behavior. In L.A. Pennington & I.A. Berg (Eds.), *An introduction to clinical psychology.* New York: Ronald Press, 1964.

Peters, H., & Jenkins, R. Improvement of chronic schizophrenic patients with guided problem-solving motivated by hunger. *Psychiatric Quarterly Supplement,* 1954, **28,** 84–101.

Peterson, D.R., Quay, H.C. & Tiffany, T.L. Personality factors related to juvenile delinquency. *Child Development,* 1961, **32,** 355–372.

Petrie, A. *Individuality in pain and suffering.* Chicago: University of Chicago Press, 1967.

Phillips, L. A social view of psychopathology. In P. London & D. Rosenhan (Eds.), *Foundations of abnormal psychology.* New York: Holt, Rinehart & Winston, 1968. Pp. 427–459.

Porteus, S.D. *Porteus maze tests: Fifty years of application.* Palo Alto: Pacific Books, 1965.

Pribram, K.H. Emotion: Toward a neuropsychological theory. In D.C. Glass (Ed.), *Neurophysiology and emotion.* New York: Rockefeller University Press, 1967. Pp. 3–40.

Quay, H.C. Dimensions of personality in delinquent boys as inferred from the factor analysis of case history data. *Child Development,* 1964, **35,** 479–484.

Quay, H.C. Personality dimensions in delinquent males as inferred from the factor analysis of behavior rating. *Journal of Research in Crime and Delinquency,* 1964, **1,** 33–37.

Quay, H.C. Psychopathic personality as pathological stimulation seeking. *American Journal of Psychiatry,* 1965, **122,** 180–183.

Quay, H.C., & Hunt, W.A. Psychopathy, neuroticism and verbal conditioning: A replication and extension. *Journal of Consulting Psychology,* 1965, **29,** 283.

Quay, H.C. & Peterson, D. The questionnaire measurement of personality dimensions associated with juvenile delinquency. Unpublished manuscript. University of Illinois, 1964.

Reed, C.F., & Cuadra, C.A. The role-taking hypothesis in delinquency. *Journal of Consulting Psychology,* 1957, **21,** 386–390.

Renner, K.E. Conflict resolution and the process of temporal integration. *Psychological Reports,* 1964, **15,** 423–438. Monograph Supplement No. 2.

Robins, Lee N. *Deviant children grown up.* Baltimore: Williams & Wilkins, 1966.

Roffwarg, H. Muzio, J., & Dement, W. Ontogenetic development of the human sleep-dream cycle. *Science,* 1966, **152,** 604–619.

Rose, R.J. Preliminary study of three indicants of arousal: Measurement, interrelationships, and clinical correlates. Unpublished doctoral dissertation. University of Minnesota, 1964.

Rotter, J.B. *Social learning and clinical psychology.* Englewood Cliffs, N.J.: Prentice-Hall, 1954.

Rubin, L.S. An organic basis for neurotic behavior. *Psychosomatics,* 1965, **6,** 220–228.

Ruch, F. *Psychology and life.* 6th ed. Chicago: Scott, Foresman, 1963.

Ruilmann, C.J., & Gulo, M.J. Investigation of autonomic responses in psychopathic personalities. *Southern Medical Journal,* 1950, **43,** 953–956.

Scarr, S. The inheritance of sociability. *American Psychologist,* 1965, **20,** 524 (Abstract).

Schachter, S., & Latané, B. Crime, cognition and the autonomic nervous system. In M.R. Jones (Ed.), *Nebraska symposium on motivation.* Lincoln: University of Nebraska Press, 1964. Pp. 221–275.

Schaffer, H.R., & Emerson, P.E. Patterns of response to physical contact in early human development. *Journal of Child Psychology and Psychiatry,* 1964, **5,** 1–13.

Schalling, D., & Levander, S. Rating of anxiety proneness and responses to electrical pain stimulation. *Scandinavian Journal of Psychology,* 1964, **5,** 1–9.

Schalling, D., & Levander, S. Spontaneous fluctuations in EDA during anticipation of pain in two delinquent groups differing in anxiety proneness. Report No. 238 from the Psychological Laboratory, University of Stockholdm, 1967.

Schalling, D., & Rosén, A. Porteus maze differences between psychopathic and non-psychopathic criminals. *British Journal of Social and Clinical Psychology,* 1968, **7,** 224–228.

Scheibel, M.E., & Scheibel, A.B. Some neural substrates of postnatal development. In M. Hoffman & L. Hoffman (Eds.), *Review of child development research.* Vol. 1. New York: Russell Sage Foundation, 1954. Pp. 481–519.

Schildkraut, J., & Kety, S. Biogenic amines and emotion. *Science,* 1967, **156,** 21–30.

Schmauk, F. A study of the relationship between kinds of punishment, autonomic arousal, subjective anxiety and avoidance learning in the primary sociopath. Unpublished doctoral dissertation. Temple University, 1968.

Schoenherr, J.C. *Avoidance of noxious stimulation in psychopathic personality.* (Doctoral dissertation, University of California, Los Angeles) Ann Arbor, Mich.: University Microfilms, 1964. No. 64–8334.

Schoper, C.A. A study of learning and retention with neutral and social-primitive words in normal, psychopathic and psychoneurotic criminals. Unpublished doctoral dissertation. University of Illinois, 1958.

Schwade, E.D., & Geiger, S.G. Abnormal electroencephalographic findings in severe behavior disorders. *Diseases of the Nervous System,* 1965, **17,** 307–317.

Schwitzgebel, R. Short-term operant conditioning of adolescent offenders on socially relevant variables. *Journal of Abnormal Psychology,* 1967, **72,** 134–142.

Shagass, C., & Schwartz, M. Observations on somatosensory cortical reactivity in personality disorders. *Journal of Nervous and Mental Disease,* 1962, **135,** 44–51.

Sherman, L.J. Retention in psychopathic, neurotic and normal subjects. *Journal of Personality,* 1957, **6,** 722–729.

Silver, A.W. TAT and MMPI psychopathic deviate scale differences between delinquent and nondelinquent adolescents. *Journal of Consulting Psychology.* 1963, **27,** 370.

Silverman, A.J., Cohen, S.I., & Shmavonian, B.M. Investigation of psychophysiologic relationships with skin resistance measure. *Journal of Psychosomatic Research,* 1959, **4,** 65–87.

Simon, B., Holzberg, J., & Unger, J. A study of judgment in the psychopathic personality. *Psychiatric Quarterly,* 1951, **25,** 132–150.

Singer, J.L. *Daydreaming.* New York: Random House, 1966.

Skrzypek, G.J. The effects of perceptual isolation and arousal on anxiety, complexity preference and novelty preference in psychopathic and neurotic delinquents. *Journal of Abnormal Psychology,* 1969, **74,** 321–329.

Sokolov, E.N. *Perception and the conditioned reflex.* New York: MacMillan, 1963.

Solomon, R.L. Letter quoted by O.H. Mowrer. *Learning theory and the symbolic processes.* New York: Wiley, 1960. Pp. 399–404.

Solomon, R.L., Turner, L.H., & Lessac, M.S. Some effects of delay of punishment on resistance to temptation in dogs. *Journal of Personality and Social Psychology,* 1968, **8,** 233–238.

Spence, J.T., & Spence, K.W. The motivational components of manifest anxiety: Drive and drive stimuli. In C.D. Spielberger (Ed.), *Anxiety and behavior.* New York: Academic Press, 1966. Pp. 291–326.

Spitzer, R., Cohen, J., Fleiss, J., & Endicott, J. On quantification of agreement in psychiatric diagnosis. *Archives of General Psychiatry,* 1967, **17,** 83–87.

Stafford-Clark, D., Pond, D., & Lovett Doust, J.W. The psychopath in prison: A preliminary report of a co-operative research. *British Journal of Delinquency,* 1951, **2,** 117–129.

Stein, L. Reciprocal action of reward and punishment mechanisms. In R. Heath (Ed.), *The role of pleasure in behavior.* New York: Harper & Row, 1964. Pp. 113–139.

Stern, J.A., & McDonald, D.G. Physiological correlates of mental disease. In P.R. Farnsworth (Ed.), *Annual Review of Psychology.* Palo Alto: Annual Reviews, Inc., 1965. Pp. 225–264.

Sternbach, R. *Principles of psychophysiology.* New York: Academic Press, 1966.

Sturup, G.K. The treatment of chronic criminals. *Bulletin of the Menninger Clinic,* 1964, **28,** 229–243.

Thorne, F.C. The etiology of sociopathic reactions. *American Journal of Psychotherapy,* 1959, **13,** 319–330.

Turner, L.H., & Solomon, R.L. Human traumatic avoidance learning: Theory and experiments on the operant-respondent distinction and failure to learn. *Psychological Monographs,* 1963, **76** (40, Whole No. 539).

Vandenberg, S. Contributions of twin research to psychology. *Psychological Bulletin,* 1966, *66,* 327–352.

Van Evra, J.P., & Rosenberg, B.G. Ego strength and ego disjunction in primary and secondary psychopaths. *Journal of Clinical Psychology,* 1963, **19,** 61–63.

Warren, Anne B., & Grant, D.A. The relation of conditioned discrimination to MMPI Pd personality variable. *Journal of Experimental Psychology,* 1955, **49,** 23–27.

Wechsler, D. *The measurement and appraisal of adult intelligence* (4th ed.) Baltimore: Williams & Wilkins, 1958.

Wiesen, A.E. *Differential reinforcing effects of onset and offset of stimulation on the operant behavior of normals, neurotics and psychopaths.* (Doctoral dissertation, University of Florida) Ann Arbor, Mich.: University Microfilms, 1965. No. 65–9625.

Wiggins, J. Inconsistent socialization. *Psychological Reports,* 1968, **23,** 303–336.

Wolff, H.S. Telemetry of psychophysiological variables. In P.H. Venables and I. Martin (Eds.), *Manual of psychophysiological method.* New York: Wiley, 1967. Pp. 521–545.

Zubin, J. Classification of the behavior disorders. In P.R. Farnsworth (Ed.), *Annual review of psychology.* Palo Alto: Annual Reviews, Inc., 1967. Pp. 373–406.

AUTHOR INDEX

SUBJECT INDEX